Learn French For Adult

Beginners Book (3 in 1)

Master Reading, Writing, and Speaking
French With This Simple 3 Step Process

Worldwide Nomad

FREE GIFT

Inside this gift you'll find:

Online Pronunciation Course: Easily perfect pronunciation through an online video course for audio learners

TO CLAIM BONUS

Scan the QR Code below

OR

Visit the link below:

https://worldwidenomadbooks.com/French-opt-in

TABLE OF CONTENTS

French Grammar Workbook and Textbook For Beginners

Introduction xiii

1. Pronunciation 1

    1.1 Alphabet 2
    1.2 Diacritics 3
    1.3 Ligatures 5
    1.4 Digraphs & Trigraphs 5
    1.5 Double consonants 8
    1.6 Silent letters 8
    1.7 Liaisons 9

2. The noun in French 13

    2.1 Gender and number in French 14
    2.2 Definite and indefinite articles 18
    Special case 19
    2.3 Partitive articles 20

3. Adjectives 23

    3.1 Qualifying adjectives 24
    3.2 Demonstrative adjectives 31
    3.3 Indefinite adjectives 32
    3.4 Possessive adjectives 33
    3.5 Interrogative adjective 35
    3.6 Exclamative adjective 35
    3.7 Relative adjectives 35
    3.8 Numbers 36

4. Basic Vocabulary 51

    4.1 Greetings & Everyday expressions 52
    4.2 People & Professions 53

4.3 Places & Directions 54
4.4 Meals & Food 56
4.5 Clothing & Accessories 58
4.6 Body 59
4.7 Nature & Weather 60
4.8 Days & Months 61
4.9 Colors & Adjectives 61

5. Present indicative (part 1) **67**
5.1 Personal pronouns 68
5.2 First-group verbs 69
5.3 Second-group verbs 73

6. Present indicative (part 2) **77**
6.1 Completely irregular verbs 78
6.2 -enir verbs 85
6.3 -tir verbs 86
6.4 -ouvrir, offrir, souffrir 87
6.5 -cevoir verbs 87
6.6 -ondre, -ordre, -erdre, -endre verbs 88
6.7 -eindre verbs 88
6.8 -aître verbs 89
6.9 -crire verbs 90
6.10 -uire verbs 90
6.11 Falloir, Pleuvoir 91

7. Forming complex sentences **93**
7.1 Negative sentences 94
7.2 Interrogative sentences 94
7.3 Interrogative adverbs 95
7.4 Coordinating conjunctions 97
7.5 Subordinating conjunctions 98
7.6 Prepositions 99
7.7 Adverbs 100
7.8 Tonic pronouns 103

8. Past tenses **105**
8.1 Passé composé 106

9. Future tenses **113**
9.1 Futur Proche 114

9.2 Futur Simple 114

10. Moods 119

10.1 Introduction to moods 120
10.2 Le participe 120
10.3 Le gérondif... 124
10.4 L'impératif.. 125
10.5 Le conditionnel 126
10.6 Le subjonctif 128

French Phrasebook For Beginners

Chapter 1 Greeting in French 133

The Basics 134
Start with a Greeting 134
Use Formal Titles... 135
Express Politeness 136
(Do not) Be Mindful of Time 136
Hands and Arms.. 137
Engage in Small Talk 137
Use Formal Language 137
Learn Basic Phrases in French 138
Show Genuine Interest 138
Participate in Cultural Customs.. 138

Chapter 2 Transportation 139

Buses... 140
Metros and Subways 141
Taxis and Ride-Sharing Services... 141
Common Phrases and Vocabulary 142

Chapter 3 Food and drinks 147

Chapter 4 Making friends (socializing)......................... 155

Examples of phrases for making friends................................ 156
Practice conversations for talking about making friends (socializing): 157
Cultural tips on socializing and making friends in French speaking countries................ 163

Chapter 5 Talking about the Weather **165**

Vocabulary related to weather conditions 166

Practice conversations for talking about the weather 168

Chapter 6 Accommodation, Hotels and Airbnb **175**

Chapter 7 The Shopping Experience in French-Speaking Countries **183**

Chapter 8 Drugstores and Hospital Visits in French-Speaking Countries **193**

Chapter 9 vocabulary related to various aspects of everyday life **203**

Vocabulary related to parts of the house 204

Vocabulary related to animals 205

Vocabulary related to airports 206

Vocabulary related to vacations 207

Vocabulary related to types of transport 207

Vocabulary Related To Tours 209

French Short Stories For Language Learners

Le Gardien Qui A Souffert De La Tromperie 213

The Gatekeeper Who Suffered Deceit 214

La Monnaie De La Sagesse 216

The Wisdom Currency 217

Le Célèbre Prince 219

The Celebrated Prince 220

Le Fils De La Paix 222

The Son Of Peace 223

Le Roi Cupide 225

The Greedy King 226

Le Choc Des Religions 228

The Clash Of Religions 229

La Convoitise Du Trône 231

Coveting The Throne 232

Contes De Laye Le Voyageur 234

Tales Of Laye The Traveler 235

Amélie Au Grand Cœur 237

Kindhearted Amelie 238

L'amour Au Temps Des Révolutions 240

Love In The Time Of Revolutions 241

Le Petit Royaume De Ruth 243

Ruth's Little Kingdom 244

La Quête Du Pouvoir 246

Quest For Power 247

Napoléon Patriote 249

Patriotic Napoleon 250

Les Princes Indignes 252

The Unworthy Princelings 253

Joan La Série 255

Joan The Seer 256

Le Cœur Rebelle D'eloise 258

Eloise's Rebellious Heart 259

La Résistance Vers La Liberté 261

Resistance Unto Freedom 262

D'ennemis À Amis 264

Enemies To Friends 265

Grande Nation, Grand Peuple 267

Great Nation, Great People 268

Courtier De La Paix 270

Peace Broker 271

Conclusion **273**

French Grammar Workbook and Textbook For

Beginners

Learn French With Essential,
Easy to Understand Lessons

Worldwide Nomad

Introduction

Welcome to your French learning manual!

Today, French is the second most-learned language in the world, with 82 million learners, and the sixth most-spoken language in the world, with over 274 million speakers. French is also the official language of 29 countries worldwide, and The Organisation Mondiale de la Francophonie, which promotes the learning and use of French around the world, comprises 88 countries on five continents.

Thus, learning French means being able to communicate with millions of people around the world, having access to one of the greatest cultural heritages of the Western world and beyond, as well as enjoying the work of philosophers, novelists, filmmakers or songwriters in their original language.

Let's face it: learning French isn't always easy. Its random noun genders, convoluted conjugation and eccentric spelling are proverbial. But this degree of sophistication, shared with the other Romance languages, is also what gives French its charm and originality, as the language of love and diplomacy.

This guide will take you step by step through the process of learning French, from pronunciation to vocabulary, from grammar to conjugation. Wherever possible, we'll also try to give you the English translation of the French words used in this manual.

By the end of your journey, you'll be able to express yourself accurately and be understood by another French speaker. With this solid foundation, you'll just have to expand your vocabulary and knowledge to quickly achieve complete fluency.

So, are you ready to learn?

1. Pronunciation

The pronunciation of French is often regarded by learners as absurd and incomprehensible. Unlike other languages, French is not always pronounced as it is written. *Digraphs* abound, as do silent letters. But, as you'll see, French is no less rational, and once you've assimilated the main principles of its particular phonetics, its pronunciation should hardly be a problem.

1.1 Alphabet

Just like English, French uses the modern Latin alphabet, composed of 26 letters. The main difference lies in the use of a special *grapheme*, five *diacritics* and two *ligatures*.

Let's start by learning how to pronounce the 26 basic letters:

Letter	Name	Pronunciation (IPA)	Equivalent (English)	Example (French)
A	Ah	a	Pat	Mardi Gras
B	Beh	b-	**B**lind	**B**leu
C	Seh	k- (usually) s- (before e,i,y) g- (rare)	**C**all **S**eed **G**ame	**C**oup **C**elui Se**c**ond
D	Deh	d-	**D**ay	**D**oute
E	Uh	ə e ɛ none (silent)	**A**bout **M**ay B**e**st -	L**e** Pi**e**d G**e**l Tass**e**
F	Eff	f-	**F**amily	**F**ou
G	Zheh	g- (usually) ʒ- (before e,i,y)	**G**ame Mea**s**ure	**G**ain **G**el
H	Ash	none (silent)	-	**H**eure
I	Ee	i	B**i**t	L**i**tre
J	Zhee	ʒ-	Mea**s**ure	**J**onjour
K	Kah	k-	**K**idney	**K**ayak
L	El	l-	**L**amp	**L**itre
M	Em	m-	**M**anual	**M**er
N	En	n-	**N**ature	**N**euf
O	Oh	o ɔ	N**o**te N**o**t	P**o**se C**o**de
P	Peh	p-	**P**ound	**P**inte
Q	/ky/ (see below)	k-	**K**idney	**Q**atar

R	Air	ʁ- ("guttural R")	Loch (Scottish English)	**R**oute
S	Ess	s- z- (between two vowels)	**S**eed Rea**s**on	**S**ale Mai**s**on
T	Teh	t- (usually) s- (before i)	**T**rick **S**eed	**T**able Produc**t**ion
U	/y/ (see below)	y	-	Tr**u**c
V	Veh	v-	**V**acant	**V**ente
W	Doo-bluh-veh ("*double V*")	v- w-	**V**acant **W**eb	**W**agon Sand**w**ich
X	Eeks	ks- gz- z- s- (rare)	Fi**x** E**x**ample Rea**s**on **S**eed	Ma**x**imum E**x**ister Di**x**ième Si**x**
Y	Ee-grek ("*Greek i*")	i (vowel use) j- (consonant use)	B**i**t **Y**ard	R**y**thme **Y**aourt
Z	Zed	z-	**Z**ero	**Z**èbre

Note on the pronunciation of the letter U (and Q): The sound of the vowel U is absent from most languages. In the International Phonetic Alphabet (IPA), it is represented by the symbol /y/. To pronounce this vowel correctly, say "eee" (like the French i) continuously and then, without stopping, tighten your mouth until you form a small circle with your lips. This is how you pronounce the letter U. The letter Q itself is pronounced **/ky/** (k- sound + /y/), but within a word, it is pronounced just like a K, as in the word *Qatar*.

Note on the general pronunciation of French: Remember at all times that the pronunciation of French changes drastically depending on the combination of letters (*digraphs*, *trigraphs*), and their position within the word. For example, the word *oiseau* (bird) is pronounced wa-zo. Also, as you'll learn in the following pages, many theoretically sound letters become silent in certain contexts. Thus, the table above describes only the basic pronunciation of French letters, which includes numerous additional rules and exceptions. English phonetic equivalents do not always correspond exactly to the actual French pronunciation. It is therefore essential to:

* Familiarize yourself with the IPA symbols used throughout this manual.
* Use audio material to supplement the written content of the book.

1.2 Diacritics

Diacritics are small graphic signs placed around a letter (usually above it) to change the way it sounds. French uses five diacritics : three *accents*, a *two dots* diacritic and a *subscript curl*.

- The *accent aigu* (acute accent), used only on the e: **é**.
- The *accent grave* (grave accent), used on a, e and u: **à, è, ù**.
- The *accent circonflexe* (circumflex accent), used on a, e, i, o and u: **â, ê, î, ô, û**.
- The *tréma* (trema), used on e, i, u and y (in proper nouns only): **ë, ï, ü, ÿ**.
- The *cédille* (cedilla), used only below the letter C to form the *C cédille* (c cedilla): **ç**.

Let's now look at how to pronounce the thirteen accented vowels and the *c cédille* grapheme.

Letter	Name	Pronunciation (IPA)	Equivalent (English)	Example (French)
À	A accent grave	a	p**a**t	déj**à**
Â	A accent circonflexe	a	p**a**t	**â**ne
É	E accent aigu	e	m**ay**	degr**é**
È	E accent grave	ɛ	b**e**st	m**è**re
Ê	E accent circonflexe	ɛ	b**e**st	for**ê**t
Ë	E tréma	ɛ / silent	b**e**st / –	no**ë**l / aigu**ë**
Î	I accent circonflexe	i	b**i**t	ab**î**me
Ï	I tréma	i	b**i**t	mosa**ï**que
Ô	O accent circonflexe	o	n**o**te	h**ô**pital
Ù	U accent grave	(see below)		o**ù**
Û	U accent circonflexe	y	–	m**û**re
Ü	U tréma	y / ɔ	– / n**o**t	Emma**ü**s / Capharna**ü**m
Ç	C cédille	s-	**s**eed	fran**ç**ais

As you can see, French diacritics do not produce any sounds that aren't already present in the basic alphabet. Most of the time, their function is to clarify the pronunciation of a word when it's ambiguous — to avoid, for example, pronouncing two independent vowels as a *digraph* (see chapter 1.4) — or to distinguish two homophones (words with identical pronunciation) in writing.

Note on the *accent circonflexe*: The circumflex accent often replaces a letter that has disappeared because it had become silent over time. The most famous case is the letter S. Thus, Old French hospital became hôpital, forest became forêt and tempeste became tempête.

Note on the *U accent grave* and the *U tréma*: The *U accent grave* is only used in one word: Où (where), which is pronounced like the digraph OU (see 1.4). The *U tréma* is mainly used in proper nouns or as an alternative to the *e tréma* in words ending in -guë. For example, the word aiguë can also be written aigüe — the pronunciation remains the same.

1.3 Ligatures

A ligature is the joining of two letters to form a single character, and a single sound. French has two ligatures: **æ** (*e-dans-l'a*) and **œ** (*e-dans-l'o*). Let's see how they are pronounced.

Ligature	Name	Pronunciation (IPA)	Equivalent (English)	Example (French)
Æ	e-dans-l'a	e	may	ex-æquo
Œ	e-dans-l'o	œ	bird	cœur
		ø	about	vœu
		ɛ	best	fœtus

Note: The Æ ligature is very rare and is mainly found in expressions of Latin origin — *Ad vitam æternam, Curriculum vitæ, Et cætera* — as well as in Læticia, a female name also of Latin origin.

1.4 Digraphs & Trigraphs

A *digraph* is a combination of two letters that form a single sound, independent of the two letters that make it up. A trigraph is the same thing, but with three letters. As an English speaker, you're already familiar with many digraphs and trigraphs, such as *ai* (as in the words *pair* or *chair*) or *igh* (as in **high** or **thigh**). French works the same way, but with different digraphs and trigraphs.

Here are the main ones:

Digraph / Trigraph	Pronunciation (IPA)	Equivalent (EN)	Example (FR)
ai, aî	ɛ	b**e**st	**pai**re, ma**î**tre
aim (at the end of a word)	ɛ̃	p**an**ts	f**aim**
ain (at the end of a word or before a consonant, except m, b or p)	ɛ̃	p**an**ts	p**ain**, m**ain**tenance
am (before b or p)	ã	w**an**t	**am**ple

an (at the end of a word or before a consonant, except m, b or p)	ã	want	plan, France
aon (at the end of a word)	ã	want	paon, faon
aou, aoû	u	too	saoul, août
au	o	note	automatique
ay	ɛj / pe-i	play / -	payer / pays
aye	e-i	-	abbaye
ch	ʃ- / k-	wash / charisma	chemin / chorale
eau	o	note	oiseau
ei	ɛ	best	neige
eim	ɛ̃	pants	Reims
ein (at the end of a word or before a consonant, except m, b or p)	ɛ̃	pants	peintre
em (before m, b or p)	ã	want	exemple
en (at the end of a word or before a consonant, except m, b or p)	ã	want	ensemble
en (at the end of a word, when preceded by an é or an i)	ɛ̃	pants	bien
er (sometimes, at the end of a word)	e	may	manger
et (at the end of a word)	ɛ	best	poulet
ez (at the end of a word)	e	may	nez
eu, eû	œ / ø / y	bird / about / -	jeune / deux, jeûne / eu, eût
ge	ʒ-	measure	page
gn	ɲ	canyon	champagne
gu	g- / gɥ- / gw-	game / - / guam	guerre / aiguille / guacamole
il (after a, e, u, œ or ue)	j	yes	ail, œil
il (before s, m, or at the end of a word)	i	bit	gentil, fils

ill (after a consonant, e, eu, œ, ou, u, or ue)	j	**ye**s	f**ill**e, ta**ill**e
ill (sometimes, after a consonant)	l	**ill**	v**ill**e
im (before m, b or p)	ɛ̃	p**an**ts	s**im**ple
in (at the end of a word or before a consonant, except m, b or p)	ɛ̃	p**an**ts	v**in**
oê	wa	**wa**cky	p**oê**le
oi, oî	wa	**wa**cky	r**oi** b**oî**te
oin	wɛ̃	-	l**oin**
om (at the end of a word, or before m, b or p)	õ	d**on**'t	n**om**, c**om**bat
on (at the end of a word, or before a consonant, except m, b or p)	õ	d**on**'t	garç**on**, rép**on**se
ou, où, oû	u	t**oo**	gen**ou**, **où**, g**oû**t
ou (before a vowel)	w-	s**w**eat	j**ou**et, **ou**i
ph	f-	**f**amily	**ph**ilosophie
qu	k- kw-	**k**idney **qu**iz	le**qu**el a**qu**atique
sch	ʃ- sk-	wa**sh** **sk**ate	**sch**éma **sch**izophrène
ss	s-	**s**eed	adre**ss**e
ue	œ	**a**bout	c**ue**illir
um	ɛ̃ ɔm*	p**an**ts bloss**om**	h**um**ble rh**um**
un (at the end of a word or before a consonant, except m, b or p)	ɛ̃	p**an**ts	**un**, empr**un**t
ym (at the end of a word or before a consonant except n)	ɛ̃	p**an**ts	th**ym**, s**ym**pathique
yn (before a consonant)	ɛ̃	p**an**ts	s**yn**drome, l**yn**x

Note: The sounds /ɑ̃/, /õ/ and /ɛ̃/, typical of the French language, are called **nasal vowels**.

To keep it in mind, you can remember the following phrase:
Un bon vin blanc (ɛ̃ bõ vɛ̃ blɑ̃ ; meaning: a good white wine).

*Note on words ending in -UM: Apart from the word *rhum*, pronunciation in -ɔm mainly concerns words borrowed from Latin: *album, forum, maximum, géranium...*

1.5 Double consonants

Good news! Unlike other languages (e.g. Spanish), most double consonants are pronounced exactly like single consonants, **except when a double consonant is part of a trigraph** (example: ill). Thus, the word *salle* (room) is pronounced exactly like the word *sale* (dirty). There are two exceptions to this rule: double c (sometimes) and double s:

Double consonant	Pronunciation (IPA)	Equivalent (English)	Example (French)
cc	k-	a**cc**ount	o**cc**asion
cc (before e and i)	ks-	a**cc**ess	su**cc**ès
ss	s-	**s**eed	poi**ss**on

1.6 Silent letters

One of the most difficult features of the French language for a learner to master are the silent letters, especially **at the end of words**. French is not a phonetic language, and many of the letters present in the written form of words aren't pronounced orally, either because they are part of a digraph or trigraph (see 1.4), or because their pronunciation has simply become silent over time.

The following letters, when placed **at the end of a word**, are usually **pronounced**:

Letter	Examples (FR)	Some exceptions (FR)
B	Club, snob, pub*	Plomb
C	Avec, bac, truc	Banc, blanc, flanc, porc, estomac, tabac
F	Chef, œuf, juif	Nerf, clef, bœufs, œufs
G	Grog, iceberg, viking	Bourg, poing, sang, long
K	Kayak, rock, trek	-
L	Avril, fil, pluriel	(cf. digraph il)
M	Tram, totem, forum	(cf. digraphs om, um, ym)
Q	Cinq, coq	-
R	Amer, cher, venir	(cf. digraph er)

*Note on words ending in B: These words are usually borrowed from other languages (usually English). Their pronunciation in French then follows the pronunciation of their original language. For example, *club* is pronounced /klœb/, not /klyb/. The same logic applies to loanwords in general, with the notable exception of the word *shampooing* (shampoo), which is pronounced /ʃɑ̃pwɛ̃/.

Now, the following letters, when placed **at the end of a word**, are usually **silent**:

Letter	Examples (FR)	Some exceptions (FR)
E (unaccented)*	Homme, livre, suite	Two-letter words: Je, ce, le...
D	Boulevard, froid, grand	Sud, snowboard
P	Beaucoup, champ, loup	Cap, rap, stop
S*	Dessus, trois, temps	Bonus, bus, fils
T	Et, objet, petit	But, contact, huit
X*	Deux, flux, prix	Dix, six, fax
Z	Assez, chez, riz	Gaz, buzz, show-biz

Note on the letter E: The letter E is by far the most common silent letter in French. It's often found at the end of words, where it's almost never pronounced. In the middle of a word, it's also common not to pronounce it. Thus, *vêtements* (clothes) is pronounced /vɛtmɑ̃/.

Note on the letter S: In addition to the examples of singular words given in the table above, you should keep in mind that, as in English, the final S is the mark of the plural form. The S marking the plural in French is always silent. On the other hand, in words borrowed from Latin, the final S is always pronounced: *bonus, utérus, virus...*

Note on the letter X: As we'll see later, some French words take an X in the plural. As with the letter S, this X is always silent. Once again, the final X is always pronounced in words of Latin origin: *cortex, lynx, thorax...*

1.7 Liaisons

In addition to the notions explained above, French pronunciation also varies according to the sequence of words in a sentence. The rule is simple: when one word ends with **a silent consonant** and the next word begins with **a vowel** or **a silent H,** the final consonant of the first word is **heard at the start of the second word**, sometimes in a slightly different form.

→ When one word ends with **a silent S** and the next begins with **a vowel** or **a silent H,** the final S of the first word turns into a **Z** sound at the start of the second word.

Example: *Mes yeux (my eyes)*
Pronunciation: *Mes (me) + yeux (jø) = mes yeux (me zjø)*

→ When one word ends with **a silent X** and the next begins with **a vowel** or **a silent H,** the final X of the first word turns into a **Z** sound at the start of the second word.

Example: *Deux amis (two friends)*

Pronunciation: *Deux (dø) + amis (ami) = deux amis (dø ẕami)*

→ When one word ends with **a silent R** and the next begins with **a vowel** or **a silent H**, the final R of the first word turns into a guttural **R** sound (ʁ) at the start of the second word.

Example: *Mon premier enfant (my first child)*
Pronunciation: *Premier (pʁəmje) + enfant (ãfã) = premier enfant (pʁəmje ʁãfã)*

→ When one word ends with **a silent T** and the next begins with **a vowel** or **a silent H**, the final T of the first word turns into a **T** sound at the start of the second word.

Example: *Tout à fait (absolutely)*
Pronunciation: *Tout (*tu*) + à (a) + fait (fɛ) = Tout à fait (tu ta fɛ)*

→ When one word ends with **a silent D** and the next begins with **a vowel** or **a silent H**, the final D of the first word turns into a **T** sound at the start of the second word.

Example: *Un grand animal (a big animal)*
Pronunciation: *Grand (*grã*) + animal (animal) = grand animal (gʁã tanimal).*

→ When one word ends with **a silent P** and the next begins with **a vowel** or **a silent H**, the final P of the first word turns into a **P** sound at the start of the second word.

Example: *Trop heureux (too happy)*
Pronunciation: *Trop (tʁo) + heureux (œʁø) = Trop heureux (tʁo pœʁø).*

→ When one word ends with **a silent N** and the next begins with **a vowel** or **a silent H**, the final N of the first word turns into a **N** sound at the start of the second word.

Example: *Un homme (a man)*
Pronunciation: *Un (ɛ̃) + homme (ɔm) = Un homme (ɛ̃ nɔm).*

Special case: nasal vowels

When a word ending with a nasal vowel (/ã/, /õ/, /ɛ̃/) and the letter N (examples: aucun, bon, bien, certain, plein...) is followed by **a vowel** or **a silent H**, two pronunciations are possible:

→ Either the nasal vowel is maintained and the following word preceded by an N.
Example: *aucun effort (no effort) > okœ̃ nefɔʁ*

Here are the main words ending with a nasal vowel and the letter N that maintain their nasal pronunciation when followed by a word beginning with a vowel or a silent h: *aucun, bien, rien, en, on, un, mon, ton, son.*

→ Or the nasal vowel is "broken" and the following word preceded by an N.
Example: *Bon appétit > bɔ **napeti***

Most of the words ending with a nasal vowel and an N actually follow this second rule: *bon, prochain, certain, plein, ancien, moyen...*

Special case: the H aspiré

Although the H is always silent in French, some words beginning with an H do not allow the liaison, a phenomenon called *H aspiré* (aspirated H). The two successive words must be pronounced independently, according to their usual pronunciation.

Exemple: *Les hiboux (The owls)*
Pronunciation: *Les (le) + hiboux (ibu) = Les hiboux (le ibu)* > No *liaison*.

Here is a list of the main words beginning with an H aspiré:

hache, haine, hall, halle, halte, hamac, hamburger, hameau, hamster, hanche, hand-ball, handicapé, hangar, harcèlement, harem, hareng, haricot, harpe, harpon, hasard, hâte, haut, hauteur, hérisson, héron, héros, heurt, hibou, hic, hiérarchie, hip-hop, hippie, hobby, hochet, hockey, hold-up, hollandais, homard, hongrois, honte, hoquet, hors, hot dog, houx, hublot, hurlement, hutte.

Additional note on *liaisons*: Depending on the context, a liaison may be required, optional or forbidden. But don't panic! We'll discover these rules step by step in the following chapters.

Exercises

Phew! That's the end of this very dense first chapter. Don't worry if you've missed out on some of the concepts: we'll be sure to repeat and revise them in the chapters to come. In the meantime, here are a few exercises to brush up on your knowledge.

1. Which of the following statements about French pronunciation are false? (several possible choices)

a)   The letter K is always pronounced the same way.
b)   The *C cédille* and the double S are pronounced differently.
c)   The *accent grave* changes the pronunciation of the letter A.
d)   The pronunciation of a letter can change radically when it's part of a digraph.
e)   Loanwords usually follow the pronunciation of their original language.
f)   When indicating the plural form, the S at the end of the word is pronounced.
g)   The digraphs *au*, *eu* and *ou* are all pronounced the same.

2. Link the following words to their respective homonyms (words that are pronounced the same).

Poil	Air
Malle	Seau
Faire	Cher
Saut	Haut
Vers	Coût
Ère	Voix
Eau	Mal
Coup	Fer
Chair	Vert
Voie	Poêle

3. Find the odd one out in each list.

a) Poisson, Glaçon, Son, Tension, Raison, Potion.
b) Vœu, Lieu, Le, Heureux, Jeûne, Pierre.
c) Parfum, Dessin, Album, Brun, Thym, Sein.
d) Genoux, Latex, Reflux, Prix, Choix, Jaloux.
e) Colle, Fille, Mule, Bol, Dalle, Nul.
f) Près, Arrêt, Volet, Noël, Paire, Nez.
g) Blanc, Frein, Sang, Gland, Vent, Plan.

4. Find the wrong *liaisons* and fix them.

a)	Les africains	>	le zafʁikɛ̃
b)	Un bon homard	>	ɛ̃ bɔ **n**ɔmaʁ
c)	Certains hommes	>	sɛʁtɛ̃ zɔm
d)	Un puissant éléphant	>	ɛ̃ pɥisã **d**elefã
e)	Trop ancien	>	tʁo **p**ãsjɛ̃
f)	Les héros	>	le eʁo
g)	Moyen Âge	>	mwajɛ̃ **n**aʒ

2. The noun in French

As in other Romance languages (Italian, Spanish, Portuguese, Romanian), nouns in French vary in gender and number. They can then be modified by articles or adjectives — masculine, feminine, singular or plural as well.

2.1 Gender and number in French

French nouns are based on a two-gender system:

- *Masculin* (masculine)
- *Féminin* (feminine)

Unlike other languages (German, Greek, Russian...) there is no neutral gender in French, which means that all the realities of this world, whether living creatures, inanimate objects or abstract concepts, belong to either the masculine or feminine gender.

Is there any way to guess the gender of a name?

In the absence of an article, adjective or contextual element, there's no way to guess the gender of a noun in French. The only thing we can say is that **words ending in E are often feminine**, but, as usual in French, there are many exceptions!

Is there any connection between a noun and its gender?

The connection between a name and its gender does sometimes make sense, for example:

- *Homme* (man, /ɔm/) is a masculine noun.
- *Femme* (woman, /fam/) is a feminine noun.

But most of the time, there is no logical link between the gender of a noun and the reality it designates. This is the case with objects and even animals, some of which are designated by only one gender, even if the species in question does, of course, include males and females!

Here are a few examples:

- *Pain* (bread) is a masculine noun.
- *Maison* (house) is a feminine noun.
- *Poisson* (fish) is a masculine noun.
- *Souris* (mouse) is a feminine noun.

However, to name living creatures, French often use different nouns for males and females. This is the case, of course, for humans (*homme/femme*), but also for many animals, such as:

- *Cheval* (horse) > *Jument* (mare).
- *Cerf* (deer) > *Biche* (hind).
- *Coq* (rooster) > *Poule* (hen).
- *Lièvre* (hare) > *Hase* (doe).
- *Porc* (hog) > *Truie* (sow).

Most of the time, the feminine of a noun is formed by adding an **E** after the masculine noun. This applies to animals, but also to professions, for instance. For phonetic reasons, feminized nouns sometimes undergo further minor changes, such as doubling the final consonant, adding or shifting an accent. Here are a few examples:

- *Renard* (male fox) > *Renarde* (female fox).
- *Chien* (male dog) > *Chienne* (female dog).
- *Chat* (male cat) > *Chatte* (female cat).
- *Loup* (male wolf) > *Louve* (female wolf).

- *Avocat* (male lawyer) > *Avocate* (female lawyer).
- *Écrivain* (male novelist) > *Écrivaine* (female novelist).
- *Employé* (male employee) > *Employée* (female employee).
- *Boulanger* (male baker) > *Boulangère* (female baker).
- *Musicien* (male musician) > *Musicienne* (female musician).

Some nouns follow more elaborate patterns:

- *Acteur* (male actor) > *Actrice* (female actor).
- *Danseur* (male dancer) > *Danseuse* (female dancer).
- *Maître* (male teacher) > *Maîtresse* (female teacher).
- *Héros* (male hero) > *Héroïne* (female hero).
- *Dieu* (male god) > *Déesse* (goddess).

⚠ The H in *hero* is aspirated, but the H in *héroïne* is silent!

Some professions admit several feminine forms:

- *Docteur* (male doctor) > *Docteur, Docteure, Doctoresse* (female doctor).
- *Auteur* (male author) > *Auteur, Auteure, Autrice* (female author).
- *Peintre* (male painter) > *Peintre, Peintresse* (female painter).

Some professions are said to be *epicene*, meaning that the masculine and feminine forms are identical. These are generally professions whose masculine form already ends in an E:

- *Juge* (male judge) > *Juge* (female judge).
- *Architecte* (male architect) > *Architecte* (female architect).
- *Maire* (male mayor) > *Maire* (female mayor).

Last but not least, a few professional nouns exist only in the feminine form. The men who practise these professions are therefore named as if they were women, including the article.

Those nouns are: *sentinelle, vigie, recrue, vedette.*

The Plural Form

Now that you've understood how gender works and how it's formed in French, let's have a look at the plural form. As English speakers, the French plural shouldn't be too much of a problem for you, as its formation is very similar to English.

→ In the plural, most French nouns, either masculine or feminine, simply take **a (silent) S**.
Examples: *homme > hommes, danseuse > danseuses, pain > pains, maison > maisons.*

→ If a singular noun ends with **an S, an X or a Z**, both spelling and pronunciation (whether sound or silent) remain the same in the plural form.
Examples: *souris > souris, prix > prix, nez > nez.*

→ If a singular noun ends in **-eu**, **-œu**, **-eau**, or **-au**, the plural ends **with a (silent) X**.
Examples: *jeu > jeux, vœu > vœux, bateau > bateaux, joyau > joyaux.*
Notable exceptions: *bleu > bleus, pneu > pneus.*

→ If a singular noun ends in **-al**, the plural will end in **-aux** (the X is silent).
Examples: *cheval > chevaux, métal > métaux, journal > journaux.*
Notable exceptions: *bal, carnaval, chacal, festival, récital, régal.*

Special cases

→ A few nouns ending in **-ail** form their plural in **-aux**.
These nouns are: *corail, bail, émail, soupirail, travail, vantail,* and *vitrail.*
Examples: *corail > coraux, travail > travaux, vitrail > vitraux.*

All the other nouns ending in -ail simply take an S.
Examples: *portail > portails, détail > détails, rail > rails.*

→ A few nouns ending in **-ou** form their plural in **-oux** (the X is silent).
These nouns are: *bijou, caillou, chou, genou, hibou, joujou* and *pou.*
Examples: *bijou > bijoux, caillou > cailloux, genou > genoux.*

→ Three nouns are regular in spelling, but their pronunciation changes in the plural:
- ○ *Os* (ɔs) > *os* (o).
- ○ *Bœuf* (bœf) > *bœufs* (bø).
- ○ *Œuf* (œf) > *œufs* (ø).

→ One noun changes completely from singular to plural:
- ◦ *Œil* (œj) > *yeux* (jø).

→ Loanwords usually follow the rules of their original language.
Examples: *Tennis**man*** > *Tennis**woman***, *Médi**um*** > *Médi**a***.

→ Acronyms are invariable, unless they formally entered the language.
Examples: (the) GMOs > les OGM, (the) UFOs > les ovnis.

What gender for a group made up of both men and women?

La loi est dure, mais c'est la loi («The law is harsh, but it is the law»): if a given group of animals is made up of both male and female, or a group of people made up of both men and women, you must always opt for the **masculine plural**, even if female/women are more numerous within the group. Only groups composed exclusively of female/women use the feminine plural (of course, this rule does not apply to nouns that don't have a masculine form, nor to epicene nouns).

Example:
- A group of lawyers, composed of two women and six men > *Les avocats*.
- A group of lawyers, composed of six women and six men > *Les avocats*.
- A group of lawyers, composed of six women and two men > *Les avocats*.
- A group of lawyers, composed of six women and no men > *Les avoca**tes***.

What nouns must be capitalized in French?

Capitalization in French is rarer than in English. Uppercase letters are called *majuscules*, lowercase letters are called *minuscules*. Capital letters are used only:

- At the beginning of a sentence: *Bonjour ! Ça va ?* (Hello! How are you?)
- For proper nouns: *Emmanuel Macron, Berlin, l'océan Atlantique...*
- For nationality nouns: *les Japonais, les Canadiens...*

⚠ Unlike in English, you must **not** capitalize:

- Months and days of the week: *lundi 5 décembre* (Monday, December 5).
- Languages: *le français, le chinois, le russe, l'italien…*
- Nationality adjectives: *un musicien <u>a</u>méricain*.
- Religions: *le christianisme, le judaïsme…* (except: *l'Islam*).
- Religious nouns: *les chrétiens, les juifs…*
- Religious adjectives: *un ami chrétien, un philosophe juif…*
- First person singular pronoun: *Oui, je suis là* (Yes, I'm here).

2.2 Definite and indefinite articles

Now that you've mastered the rules of gender and number in French, it's time to discover the other words that evolve around nouns and specify their meaning. These different types of words are the same as in English, except that they vary in gender and number, following the inner logic of the French language. Let's start with the articles.

Articles are short words placed before a noun to specify if this noun is specific or not.
- **Definite articles** indicate that the noun is a **specific** person, animal or thing.
- **Indefinite articles** indicate that the noun is an **unspecified** person, animal or thing.

Here are the different articles in French:

	Masculine	Feminine
Singular definite	Le, L'	La, L'
Plural definite	Les	
Singular indefinite	Un	Une
Plural indefinite	Des	

→ Before a vowel or a silent H, the singular definite article, either masculine or feminine, becomes **L'** (*L apostrophe*), a phenomenon known as *élision* (elision). Before an aspirated H, the usual definite articles are used: le, la.

→ Before an aspirated H, the feminine singular indefinite article (une), usually pronounced /yn/ is often pronounced **/ynœ/**. Thus, *une hache* (an axe) would be pronounced /ynœ aʃ/.

⚠ Pay attention to the *liaisons*! Reread Chapter 1.7 if necessary.

Here are a few examples to help you understand:

Masculine singular definite article: le pain, l'horizon, l'oiseau, le hibou, l'os.
Masculine plural definite article: les pains, les horizons, les oiseaux, le hibou, les os.

Feminine singular definite article: la maison, l'heure, l'avocate, la hanche.
Feminine plural definite article: les maisons, les heures, les avocates, les hanches.

Masculine singular indefinite article: un homme, un chat, un corail, un médium, un œuf.
Masculine plural indefinite article: des hommes, des chats, des coraux, des média, des œufs.

Feminine singular indefinite article: une femme, une louve, une avocate, une souris.
Feminine plural indefinite article: des femmes, des louves, des avocates, des souris.

Special case

When an **adjective** precedes the noun, the plural indefinite article des becomes **de** before a consonant or an aspirated H, or **d'** before a vowel or a silent H (elision):

*   *Des femmes* (women) > *De belles femmes* (beautiful women).
*   *Des secrets* (secrets) > *De honteux secrets* (shameful secrets).
*   *Des villes* (cities) > *D'affreuses villes* (hideous cities).
*   *Des guerriers* (warriors) > *D'héroïques guerriers* (heroic warriors).

When to use definite articles?

→ Definite articles serve to designate something or someone **specific**.

For example: *J'ai vendu la voiture (I sold the car)*.

In this sentence, the speaker is mentioning a specific car, presumably known to the person to whom the sentence is addressed.

→ Definitive articles are also used to state **generalities**.
For example: *Les chiens sont fidèles (Dogs (in general) are loyal)*.

⚠ Unlike in English, you **must** use definite articles before:

*   **Countries**: *La France, le Canada, les États-Unis*.
*   **Languages**: *Le français, l'anglais, le japonais*.
*   **Concepts**: *L'amour, la patience, les mathématiques*.

When to use indefinite articles?

→ Indefinite articles are used to designate an **indeterminate** person or thing.

For example: *J'ai vendu une voiture* (I sold a car).

Here, the speaker doesn't specify which car he's talking about, and we assume that the person he's talking to doesn't know either.

⚠ Unlike in English, **do not** use indefinite articles before:

*   **Professions**: *Elle est avocate* (She is a lawyer).
*   **Religions:** *Je suis catholique* (I'm a Catholic).

Except if the noun is preceded by an adjective:

C'est une célèbre avocate (She's a famous lawyer).
Je suis un bon catholique (I'm a good Catholic).

2.3 Partitive articles

Partitive articles are the third and last type of article in French.

Partitive articles are used when referring to an **uncountable quantity**.
These articles can apply to concrete objects or to more abstract notions.

Having no equivalent in English, they are usually translated by *some*, or left out entirely.

Example: *Je bois du lait* > I'm drinking (some) milk.

Here are the French partitive articles:

	Masculine	Feminine
Singular partitive	Du, de l'	De la, de l'
Plural partitive	Des	

As you can see, the pattern of partitive articles is very similar to that of indefinite articles.

→ Did you notice the *L apostrophe*? As usual, it appears before a noun beginning with a **vowel** or a **silent H**. And, as usual, nouns beginning with an aspirated H are not affected.

→ The plural partitive article applies only to nouns that express quantity in the plural form. Examples: *restes* (leftovers), *biens* (goods), *haricots* (beans), *frites* (fries).

Here are a few examples to help you understand:

Masculine singular partitive article: *du beurre* (some butter), *de l'argent* (some money), *du hareng* (some herring), *de l'honneur* (some honor).

Feminine singular partitive article: *de la salade* (some salad), *de l'eau* (some water), *de l'huile* (some oil), *de la haine* (some hatred).

Masculine plural partitive article: *des décombres* (some debris).

Feminine plural partitive article: *des frites* (some fries), *des haricots* (some beans).

Special cases

→ In the **negative form**, partitive articles become **de** before a consonant or an aspirated H, and **d'** before a vowel or a silent H (elision):

- *Tu bois du lait* (You drink milk) > *Tu ne bois pas de lait* (You don't drink milk).
- *Il mange de la viande* (He eats meat) > *Il ne mange pas de viande* (He doesn't eat meat).
- *Elle a de l'argent* (She has money) > *Elle n'a pas d'argent* (She doesn't have money).
- *Tu verses de l'huile* (You pour oil) > *Tu ne verses pas d'huile* (You don't pour oil).
- *Je veux des haricots* (I want beans) > *Je ne veux pas de haricots* (I don't want beans).

→ More on the negative form in Chapter 7.1

The same phenomenon occurs when the noun is preceded by an **adverb of quantity**:

- *Tu bois du lait* (You drink milk) > *Tu bois un peu de lait* (You drink a little milk).
- *Il mange de la viande* (He eats meat) > *Il mange beaucoup de viande* (He eats a lot of meat).

→ More on adverbs in Chapter 7.7

Exercices

1. Indicate the gender and number of the following nouns:
In some cases (un, une, le, la), the article can help you determine the gender of an unknown noun. In other cases (des, les, l') you'll have to know the gender of the noun already. Word endings can also help, but unlike articles, you can't rely on them to know the gender of a noun: some feminine nouns may look masculine, and vice versa. Wait, there's a trap! The gender of one of these ten words is impossible to determine without context. Can you find it in the list?

noun	masculine	feminine	singular	plural
ex: un chien	X		X	
des hommes				
une pomme				
l'avocate				
les chevaux				
des juges				
les heures				
l'oiseau				
des horizons				
le Canada				

2. Fill in the blank to make the noun feminine:

Un cheval   >   Une _____.
Un lapin   >   Une lap___.
Un politicien >   Une politic_____.
Un architecte >   Une archit_____.
Un serveur   >   Une serv_____.
Un directeur   >   Une direc_____.
Une vedette   >   Une _____.

3. Which of these plural nouns are incorrect?

a) *Une fermière > des fermières*
b) *Un os > des oses*
c) *Un coq > des poules*
d) *Une employée > des employées*
e) *Un canal > des canaux*
f) *Le bijou > les bijoux*
g) *L'œil > les œils*
h) *La souris > les souris*
i) *L'oiseau > les oiseaus*
j) *Le caméraman > les caméraman*

4. Correct the following incorrect sentences:

Des beaux hommes   >   __ beaux hommes.
J'aime beaucoup berlin   >   J'aime beaucoup _erlin.
Rendez-vous Lundi   >   Rendez-vous _undi.
J'adore Français   >   J'adore __ _rançais.
Elle est une Chrétienne >   Elle est _____.
Je bois de la eau   >   Je bois __ _ eau.
Tu as un peu de l'argent >   Tu as un peu _ argent.

3. Adjectives

Now that you understand and master how gender and number work in French, you shouldn't have any trouble understanding how **adjectives** work. In fact, the vast majority of adjectives simply agree in gender and number with the noun they modify.

French adjectives can be divided into three main families:

* **Qualifying** adjectives (*adjectifs qualificatifs*)
* **Non-qualifying** adjectives (*adjectifs non-qualificatifs*)
* **Verbal** adjectives (*adjectifs verbaux*)

→ A verbal adjective is actually a verbal participle used as an adjective.
We'll talk about it in Chapter 10.1, dedicated to participles.

3.1 Qualifying adjectives

Qualifying adjectives are used to describe a noun or pronoun in more detail.

Their function is very similar to that of English adjectives, except that:

* French adjectives agree in gender and number with the noun they qualify.
* French adjectives are almost always placed **after** the noun.
* French adjectives can qualify multiple nouns at once.

Adjective agreement

French adjectives have four distinct forms:

	masculine	feminine
singular	fort	forte
plural	forts	fortes

The adjective simply agrees in gender and number with the noun it modifies:

A strong man > *un homme fort*
A strong woman > *une femme forte*
Strong men > *des hommes forts*
Strong women > *des femmes fortes*

⚠ Don't forget the *liaisons*! Reread Chapter 1.7 if necessary.

The feminine form

Most adjectives ending in a **consonant** form the feminine form simply by **adding an E** at the end of the masculine. Pronunciation evolves accordingly, and sometimes significantly, pronouncing the final consonant (silent in the masculine) and sometimes «breaking» a digraph. The E itself remains **silent**.

Anglais > anglaise	/ɑ̃glɛz/
National > nationale	
Petit > petite	/pətit/
Brun > brune	/bʁyn/
Plein > pleine	/plɛn/
Sain > saine	/sɛn/
Fin > fine	/fin/

Notable exceptions

Long > longue	/lɔ̃g/
Gentil > gentille	/ʒɑ̃tij/
Épais > épaisse	/epɛs/
Gras > grasse	/gʁas/
Gros > grosse	/gʁos/
Tiers > tierce	/tjɛʁs/
Frais > fraîche	/fʁɛʃ/
Bas > basse	/bas/

Adjectives ending in **a vowel** just take a silent e.
This rule also applies to accented vowels (usually **é**).

Vrai > vraie
Joli > jolie
Nu > nue
Doué > douée

Notable exceptions

Beau > belle   /bɛl/
Jumeau > jumelle   /ʒymɛl/
Nouveau > nouvelle   /nuvɛl/
Favori > favorite   /favɔʁit/

Fo**u** > f**olle**   /fɔl/
Mo**u** > m**olle**   /mɔl/

Epicene adjectives (usually ending in -e) remain the same in masculine and feminine forms.

Sympathique > sympathique
Autonome > autonome
Célèbre > célèbre
Drôle > drôle

Adjectives ending in **-c** have a feminine form in **-che**, **-cque** or **-que**.

Blan**c** > blan**che**   /blɑ̃ʃ/
Se**c** > sè**che**   /sɛʃ/
Publi**c** > publi**que**
Tur**c** > tur**que**
Gre**c** > gre**cque**

Adjectives ending in **-f** have a feminine form in **-ve**.
Pronunciation evolves accordingly: /f/ > /**v**/

Neu**f** > neu**ve**
Acti**f** > acti**ve**
Naï**f** > naï**ve**

Adjectives ending in **-x** have a feminine form in **-se**.

Jalou**x** > jalou**se**   /ʒaluz/
Heureu**x** > heureu**se**   /œʁøz/

Notable exceptions

Dou**x** > dou**ce**   /dus/
Rou**x** > rou**sse**   /rus/
Fau**x** > fau**sse**   /fos/
Vieu**x** > vi**eille** /vjɛj/

Most adjectives ending in **-en**, **-on**, **-ot**, **-ul**, **-el**, **-iel** or **-eil** double their final consonant, then add a silent E. Pronunciation evolves accordingly. When the last consonant is an **L**, pronunciation remains the same as for the masculine form.

Ancien > Ancienne   /ãsjɛn/
Bon > Bonne   /bɔn/
Sot > Sotte   /so/ > /sɔt/
Nul > nulle
Cruel > cruelle
Officiel > officielle
Pareil > pareille

Notable exceptions

Seul > seule
Bien > bien (epicene)

Adjectives ending in **-er** have a feminine form in **-ère**.
Pronunciation evolves accordingly: /e/ > /ɛʁ/

Premier > première
Dernier > dernière
Léger > légère
Fier > fière

Adjectives ending in **-et** have a feminine form in **-ette**.
Pronunciation evolves accordingly: /ɛ/ > /ɛt/

Muet > muette
Cadet > cadette

Notable exceptions

Complet > complète
Discret > discrète
Inquiet > inquiète
Secret > secrète

Adjectives ending in **-eur** have various feminine endings.

Meilleur > meilleure
Menteur > menteuse /mãtøz/
Destructeur > destructrice / dɛstʁyktʁis/

The plural form

The formation of the plural form of adjectives in French is very simple. It follows the same logic as for nouns, except that adjectives often have a masculine and a feminine form. However, this nuance poses no particular difficulty.

→ In the vast majority of cases, the plural form of adjectives is formed by **adding a silent S** to the singular form (masculine or feminine).

Un homme fort (a strong man) > *des hommes fort**s***
Une femme forte (a strong woman) > *des femmes forte**s***

→ In terms of pronunciation, this often means that several silent letters follow one another. Thus, in the following example, all underlined letters are **silent**:

Un hom<u>me for</u>t / *des hom<u>mes forts</u>*
Une fem<u>me</u> fort<u>e</u> / *des fem<u>mes forts</u>*

⚠ When a group of words is made up of both masculine and feminine nouns, the plural adjectives qualifying them are **always in the masculine form**. If all nouns are feminine, the feminine plural is used.

Un train et un vélo bleus (a blue train and a blue bicycle)
Une voiture et un train bleus (a blue car and a blue train)
Une voiture et une maison bleues (a blue car and a blue house)

When the feminine form is pronounced differently from the masculine (e.g. fort/forte), it's preferable for the last noun in the word group to be masculine.

Des hommes et des femmes forts > *des femmes et des hommes forts* ✓

Special cases

Singular **masculine** adjectives ending in **S** or **X** remain the same in the plural.

Un gros éléphant (a big elephant) > *de gros éléphants*
Un garçon jaloux (a jealous boy) > *des garçons jaloux*

<u>but</u>

*Une gro**sse** éléphante* (a big female elephant) > *de gro**sses** éléphantes*
*Une fille jalou**se** (a jealous girl) > *des filles jalou**ses***

⚠ Have you noticed how the indefinite article **des** becomes **de** (or **d'** before a vowel or a silent H) when the adjective precedes the noun? We've already talked about this rule in Chapter 2.2.

Singular **masculine** adjectives ending in **-al** or **-eau** end in **-aux** and **–eaux** in the plural.

Un héros national (a national male hero) > *des héros nationaux*
Un nouveau livre (a new book) > *de nouveaux livres*

<u>but</u>

Une héroïne nationale (a national female hero) > *Des héroïnes nationales*
Une nouvelle maison (a new house) > *de nouvelles maisons*

Notable exceptions

banal, bancal, fatal, fractal, natal, naval, tonal take a silent S in the plural.
Ex: un village natal (a hometown) > *des villages natals*

Should I place adjectives before or after the noun?

Unlike in English, French adjectives are usually placed **after** the noun.
The following adjectives are **always** placed **after** the noun they qualify:

- **Color** adjectives
  Ex: un cheval noir, une voiture blanche, des livres bleus.

- **Shape** adjectives
  Ex: un visage rond, une maison carrée, des lunettes rectangulaires.

- **Nationality** adjectives
  Ex: un policier français, une femme thaïlandaise, des artistes japonais.

- **Religious** adjectives
  Ex: une église catholique, une famille juive, des enfants musulmans.

- Verbal adjectives based on the **past participle** of a verb.
  Ex: un artiste adoré, une horloge cassée, du saumon fumé.

- Adjectives **followed by a** <u>complement</u>.
  Ex: un détail bon <u>*à savoir*</u> (A detail worth <u>knowing</u>).

⚠ French poetry notoriously likes to invert the placement of adjectives for stylistic reasons and/or to emphasize the adjective. Example: *La claire fontaine* (The clear fountain). As a result, placing the adjective at the wrong position in French will make you sound like a poet!

Short and/or **common** adjectives are usually placed **before** the noun they qualify.

Une belle femme (a beautiful woman)
Du bon travail (some good work)
Un joli garçon (a handsome boy)
De mauvais films (bad movies)

Adjectives that don't fit into the above categories can be used before or after the noun. While the basic rule remains to place the adjective after the noun, placing the adjective before the noun would give your sentence a more formal or lyric feel.

In some cases, the position of the adjective changes its meaning:

Un homme grand (a <u>tall</u> man) ≠ *Un grand homme* (a <u>great</u> man)
Une femme pauvre (a <u>disadvantaged</u> woman) ≠ *Une pauvre femme* (a <u>pitiful</u> woman)
Un hôpital ancien (an <u>old</u> hospital) ≠ *Un ancien hôpital* (a <u>former</u> hospital)

Special cases

In order to avoid vowel hiatus, the words *beau, nouveau, fou* and *vieux* change form when placed before a noun starting with a **vowel** or a **silent H**. This rule only applies to the **masculine singular**.

Un homme beau (a beautiful man) > *Un **bel** homme*
Un équipage fou (a <u>mad</u> shipcrew) > *Un **fol** équipage* (a <u>wild</u> shipcrew)
Un ami vieux (an <u>elderly</u> friend) > Un vie**il** ami (a <u>longtime</u> friend)
Un avocat nouveau (a new lawyer) > *Un nouv**el** avocat*

Epithètes and attributs

An ***adjectif épithète*** (epithete adjective) is an adjective that directly precedes or follows a noun.

Le gros chien (the big dog)
La mer calme (the calm sea)
Les bateaux verts (the green boats)

An ***adjectif attribut*** (predicate adjective) is connected to the noun through a **stative verb**.

Le chien semble gros (the dog seems big)
La mer demeure calme (the sea remains calm)
Les bateaux sont verts (the boats are green)

→ The rules governing the gender and number agreement of qualifying adjectives apply equally to epithet and predicate adjectives.

3.2 Demonstrative adjectives

Congrats! You've now mastered the use of qualifying adjectives in French. However, there are other **non-qualifying adjectives**. Fortunately, these are easy to understand, so you shouldn't have any trouble using them.

Let's start with the **demonstrative adjectives**.

Demonstrative adjectives are used to show (literally or figuratively) a specific being or thing. They are more precise than definite articles and leave no room for doubt as to what they refer to. Demonstrative adjectives are **always** placed before the noun.

There are four demonstrative adjectives in French (but in fact, only three):

	masculine	feminine
singular	ce, cet	cette
plural	ces	

→ These demonstrative adjectives are the French equivalents of **this/that** (singular) and **these/ those** (plural). The nuance that exists in English between these words doesn't exist in French. The distinction can only be made in context.

→ To avoid hiatus, the masculine singular demonstrative adjective **ce** (/sə/) becomes **cet** (/sɛt/) before a **vowel** or a **silent H**. Its pronunciation is then identical to the feminine form **cette** (/sɛt/).

→ As is often the case in French, the plural is identical for both genders.

Ce cheval (this/that horse) > *ces chevaux* (these/those horses)
Ce hibou (this/that owl) > *ces hiboux* (these/those owls)

Cet acteur (this/that male actor) > *ces acteurs* (these/those male actors)
Cet homme (this/that man) > *ces hommes* (these/those men)

Cette infirmière (this/that female nurse) > *ces infirmières* (these/those female nurses)
Cette table (this/that table) > *ces tables* (these/those tables)

3.3 Indefinite adjectives

Indefinite adjectives are used to express a **vague** or **nil** quantity. They can also express **generality**, **identity** or **difference**. Their function is similar to that of indefinite articles, but indefinite adjectives are more various and more precise. Indefinite adjectives are **always** placed before the noun.

Here's a list of the main indefinite adjectives in French:

meaning	masculine singular	feminine singular	masculine plural	feminine plural
no	aucun	aucune	aucuns	aucunes
other	autre		autres	
some	certain	certaine	certains	certaines
each, every	chaque			
various			différents	différentes
various			divers	diverses
any	n'importe quel	n'importe quelle	n'importe quels	n'importe quelles
same	même		mêmes	
no	nul	nulle	nuls	nulles
several			plusieurs	
some, a few	quelque		quelques	
such	tel	telle	tels	telles
every, all	tout	toute	tous	toutes

→ As you can see, some indefinite adjectives can only be used in the singular, others only in the plural. Adjectives ending in -e are epicene, while others follow the usual rules for forming the feminine form (see 3.1).

Here's how to use each of these adjectives in a sentence:

Aucun homme n'a jamais marché sur Mars (No man has ever walked on Mars).

J'ai d'autres frères (I have other brothers).

Certaines voitures sont trop chères (Some cars are too expensive).

Chaque visage est unique (Every face is unique).

*Elle a rencontré **différentes** personnes* (She met <u>various</u> people).

*Ils parlent **divers** dialectes* (They speak <u>various</u> dialects).

***N'importe quel** abruti peut réussir* (<u>Any</u> idiot can succeed).

*On a les **mêmes** chaussures* (We have the <u>same</u> shoes).

***Nulle** conviction ne mérite de mourir* (<u>No</u> conviction is worth dying for).

*Vous avez **plusieurs** choix* (You have <u>several</u> choices).

*J'ai **quelques** idées pour l'ave*nir (I have <u>a few</u> ideas for the future).

*Tu n'as jamais eu de **tels** problèmes* (You've never had <u>such</u> problems).

***Toute** femme mérite le respect* (<u>Every</u> woman deserves respect).

⚠ Understanding the function of a word is essential to understanding its meaning. Used as a <u>qualifying</u> adjective, the word *certain* means «sure, definite» (ex: *une décision certaine* ; a definite decision). Used as an <u>indefinite</u> adjective, it means «some, a certain» (ex: *une certaine décision* ; a certain decision). To distinguish between the different uses of a same word, the position of the adjective in relation to the noun is crucial.

3.4 Possessive adjectives

As their name suggests, possessive adjectives are used to indicate **belonging**.

As usual in French, possessive adjectives vary in gender and number:

	masculine	feminine	plural
1st person singular	mon	ma, mon	mes
2nd person singular	ton	ta, ton	tes
3rd person singular	son	sa, son	ses
1st person plural	notre		nos
2nd person plural	votre		vos
3rd person plural	leur		leurs

⚠ Please notice that French uses a different word for the second person singular and the second person plural, depending on whether the designated object belongs to one or several persons.

→ Unlike in English, French possessive adjectives agree with the gender and number **of the thing that is possessed**. If a noun is masculine, it will always use masculine possessive adjectives, even if its possessor is a woman. If a noun is feminine, it will always use feminine possessive adjectives, even if its possessor is a man.

Here's a little story to help you understand how possessive adjectives work in French:

- Jacques (a man) has a car.
- In French, the word for car is feminine: **une** *voiture*.
- When Jacques speaks about his car, he says «**Ma** *voiture*».
- Now, Jacques sells his car to his neighbor Marie (a woman).
- When Marie speaks about her car, she says «**Ma** *voiture*» as well.
- Marie also owns a bicycle: **un** *vélo*.
- When Marie speaks about her bicycle, she says «**Mon** *vélo*».

In the plural, possessive adjectives are identical in masculine and feminine forms:

Jacques a vendu **ses** *voitures* (Jacques has sold his cars).

Marie a vendu **ses** *vélos* (Marie has sold her bicycles).

Notre *voiture* (our car) / **notre** *vélo* (our bicycle).

Nos *voitures* (our cars) / **nos** *vélos* (our bicycles).

Votre *voiture* (your (several owners) car) / **votre** *vélo* (your (several owners) bicycle).

Vos *voitures* (your (several owners) cars) / **vos** *vélos* (your (several owners) bicycles).

Leur *voiture* (their car) / **leur** *vélo* (their bicycle).

Leurs *voitures* (their cars) / **leurs** *vélos* (their bicycles).

→ To avoid vowel hiatus, feminine singular possessive adjectives (ma, ta, sa) become **mon, ton, son** (similar to the masculine forms) when placed **just before** a noun beginning with a vowel or a silent H. If an adjective beginning with a consonant or an aspirated H precedes the noun, the standard feminine possessive adjective can be used.

Ma voiture (my car) > *ma belle voiture* (my beautiful car)
Ta hache (your axe) > *ta grosse hache* (my big axe)
Mon amie (my girl friend) > *ma vieille amie* (my old girl friend)
Son histoire (my story) > *sa nouvelle histoire* (my new story)

3.5 Interrogative adjective

Interrogative adjectives are **used in questions** about the nature of a specific thing/person. There is only one interrogative adjective in French: *Quel*, equivalent to both *what* and *which*.

The interrogative adjective agrees in gender and number with the designated object:

	masculine	feminine
singular	quel	quelle
plural	quels	quelles

→ The pronunciation of the four forms of the adjective is identical (/kɛl/), except in the case of *liaison* (see Chapter 1.7).

Here are a few examples of how the interrogative adjective is used:

Quel vélo as-tu acheté ? (What/which bicycle did you buy?)
Quelle heure est-il ? (What time is it?)
Quels peintres aime-t-elle ? (Which painters does she like?)
Quelles erreurs ont-ils faites ? (What mistakes did they make?)

3.6 Exclamative adjective

The interrogative adjective can also be used to express **admiration**, **astonishment** or **indignation**. It is then called an **exclamative adjective**.

Quel beau garçon ! (What a handsome boy!)
Quelle surprise ! (What a surprise!)
Quels sales menteurs ! (What filthy liars!)
Quelles gentilles femmes ! (What nice women!)

3.7 Relative adjectives

The word *lequel* (who/which) and its various forms are most often used as pronouns. However, in rare instances, they can also be used as **relative adjectives**, to establish a relationship between a noun and another antecedent noun or fact.

	masculine	feminine
who/which (singular)	lequel	laquelle
who/which (plural)	lesquels	lesquelles

in/to which (singular)	auquel	à laquelle
in/to which (plural)	auxquels	auxquelles
of/from which/whom (singular)	duquel	de laquelle
of/from which/whom (plural)	desquels	desquelles

⚠ Relative adjectives agree **with the noun they designate**, not with the antecedent noun/fact.

Here are a few examples of how relative adjectives are used:

Le demandeur est le fils d'<u>un citoyen français,</u> <u>lequel</u> <u>citoyen</u> a quitté le pays un an avant.
The applicant is the son of <u>a French citizen,</u> <u>which</u> <u>citizen</u> had left the country a year before.

Often, the noun designated by the relative adjective is different from the antecedent noun or fact (although they designate the same thing):

Il me doit <u>1000 euros,</u> <u>laquelle</u> <u>somme</u> sera versée en liquide.
He owes me <u>1,000 euros,</u> <u>which</u> <u>sum</u> will be paid in cash.

Je risque d'<u>être en retard,</u> <u>auquel</u> <u>cas</u> commencez à manger sans moi.
I might be late, in which case start eating without me.

Elle aime <u>Maria Callas et Céline Dion,</u> <u>desquelles</u> <u>chanteuses</u> elle s'inspire.
She loves <u>Maria Callas and Céline Dion,</u> <u>singers</u> <u>from</u> <u>whom</u> she takes her inspiration.

3.8 Numbers

The last section of this chapter, simply called «numbers», actually introduces two different types of numeral adjectives:

- **Cardinal adjectives**
  These are the words used to **count** people or things: one, two, three...

- **Ordinal adjectives**
  These are the words used to indicate **order**: first, second, third...

Cardinal adjectives

Let's start with the cardinal adjectives.

Number	Masculine	Feminine	Pronunciation (IPA)
1	un	une	ɛ̃ ; yn

2	deux	dø
3	trois	tʁwa
4	quatre	katʁ
5	cinq	sɛ̃k
6	six	sis
7	sept	sɛt
8	huit	ɥit
9	neuf	nœf
10	dix	dis

→ Only the number 1 has a feminine form. Numbers from 2 to 10, as well as compound numbers that do not include the word *un* are all **epicene**.

Un homme, une femme.
Deux hommes, deux femmes.
Vingt-quatre (24) *hommes, vingt-quatre femmes.*

but

Vingt-et-un (21) *hommes, vingt-et-une femmes.*
Trente-et-un (31) *hommes, trente-et-une femmes.*
etc.

Pronunciation

⚠ Unless otherwise stated, all the following pronunciation rules also apply to compound numbers ending with the numbers in question (ex: **un**, vingt-et-**un**, trente-et-**un**, etc.).

→ The **final X** in the number *deux* is silent when the letter is pronounced alone, as well as before a consonant or an aspirated H.

Deux femmes : dø fam
Deux héros : dø eʁo

Before a vowel or a silent H, the same final X is pronounced **Z** to make the liaison.

Deux avocates : dø **z**avɔkat
Deux hommes : dø **z**ɔm

→ The same rule applies to the number *trois* and its **final S**.

Trois femmes : tʁwa fam

Trois avocates : tʁwa **z**avɔkat
Trois hommes : tʁwa **z**ɔm

→ The **final Q** in the number *cinq* is usually pronounced. However, it becomes silent in certain cases, such as before the word *minutes* or when it's part of a compound number followed by a word beginning with a consonant or an aspirated H.

Cinq secondes : sɛ̃**k** səgɔ̃d
Cinq minutes : sɛ̃ minyt
Vingt-cinq secondes (25 seconds) : vɛ̃-tsɛ̃ səgɔ̃d

→ The **final X** in the numbers *six* and *dix* is pronounced **S** when the letters are pronounced alone. It becomes silent before a consonant or an aspirated H, and is pronounced **Z** before a vowel or a silent H. Just like the X in *deux*, it's actually never pronounced X!

Six, dix : si**s**, di**s**
Six femmes : si fam
Six amis : si **z**ami
Six hommes : si **z**ɔm

→ The **final X** in the number *dix* is pronounced **Z** in the following compound numbers:

Dix-huit (18) : di-**z**ɥit
Dix-neuf (19) : di-**z**nœf

→ The **P** in the number *sept* is completely silent: sɛt.
→ The **H** in the number *huit* is always aspirated, except in compound numbers.

Un grand huit (a roller coaster) : ɛ̃ gʁɑ̃ ɥit
Dix-huit (18) : di-**z**ɥit
Vingt-huit (28) : vɛ̃-**t**ɥit

→ The **final T** in the number *huit* is pronounced **T** when the letter is pronounced alone, and before a vowel or a silent H. It becomes silent before a consonant or an aspirated H.

Huit : ɥi**t**
Huit amis : ɥi **t**ami
Huit hommes : ɥi **t**ɔm
Huit femmes : ɥi fam
Huit héros : ɥi eʁo

→ The **final F** in the number *neuf* is usually pronounced **F**. However, it is pronounced **V** before the following words: *ans, autres, heures, hommes.*

Neuf : nœf
Neuf amis : nœf ami
Neuf femmes : nœf fam
Neuf ans : nœ **vã**
Neuf autres : nœ **votʁ**
Neuf heures : nœ **vœʁ**
Neuf hommes : nœ **vɔm**

This rule also applies to all compound numbers ending with *neuf*:

Dix-neuf (19) *heures* : di-znœ **vœʁ**
Vingt-neuf (29) *hommes* : vɛ̃-tnœ **vɔm**
Soixante-neuf (69) *ans* : swasɑ̃-tnœ **vã**
etc.

Numbers from 11 to 19 present some difficulties:

Number	Masculine	Feminine	Pronunciation (IPA)
11		onze	ɔ̃z
12		douze	duz
13		treize	tʁɛz
14		quatorze	katɔʁz
15		quinze	kɛ̃z
16		seize	sɛz
17		dix-sept	di-sɛt
18		dix-huit	di-**zɥ**it
19		dix-neuf	di-**zn**œf

→ Unlike English, French has a specific word for the numbers 13, 14, 15 and 16. From 17 upwards, numbers are formed simply by adding the word for the ten and the word for the unit.

10 (*dix*) + 7 (*sept*) = *dix-sept*
10 (*dix*) + 8 (*huit*) = *dix-huit*
10 (*dix*) + 9 (*neuf*) = *dix-neuf*

Pronunciation

→ The word *onze* functions <u>as if</u> it began with an aspirated H, meaning both **liaisons and elisions are forbidden before it**. There is no exception to this rule.

Les onze hommes : le ɔ̃ zɔm
Une fille de onze ans (An eleven-year-old girl) : yn fij də ɔ̃ zɑ̃

Let's continue with the tens, from 20 to 69:

Number	Masculine	Feminine	Pronunciation (IPA)
20	vingt		vɛ̃
21	vingt-et-un	vingt-et-une	vɛ̃-te-ɛ̃ / vɛ̃-te-yn
22	vingt-deux		vɛ̃-tdø
23	vingt-trois		vɛ̃-ttʁwa
30	trente		tʁɑ̃t
40	quarante		kaʁɑ̃t
50	cinquante		sɛ̃kɑ̃t
60	soixante		swasɑ̃t
69	soixante-neuf		swasɑ̃-tnœf

Compound numbers are always formed the same way:

20 (*vingt*) + 2 (*deux*) = *vingt-deux*
49 (*quarante*) + 9 (*neuf*) = *quarante-neuf*
67 (*soixante*) + 7 (*sept*) = *soixante-sept*
etc.

The numbers 21, 31, 41, 51 and 61 are written as follows:

21: *vingt-et-un(e)* (twenty-and-one)
31: *trente-et-un(e)* (thirty-and-one)
41: *quarante-et-un(e)* (forty-and-one)
51: *cinquante-et-un(e)* (fifty-and-one)
61: *soixante-et-un(e)* (sixty-and-one)

⚠ The letter **T** in *et* (and) is always silent, even before a vowel or a silent H.

Pronunciation

→ The letter **G** in the number *vingt* is completely silent (vɛ̃).

→ The **final T** in the number *vingt* is silent when the letter is pronounced alone, before a consonant or an aspirated H. Before a vowel or a silent H, it is pronounced **T**, to make the liaison.

Vingt : vɛ̃
Vingt femmes : vɛ̃ fam

Vingt <u>h</u>éros : vɛ̃ eʁo
Vingt <u>a</u>ns : vɛ̃ **tɑ̃**
Vingt <u>h</u>eures : vɛ̃ **tœʁ**

→ However, in numbers **21 to 29**, the T is **always pronounced**, even before a consonant or an aspirated H. In the number 23, the **two T's** must be clearly pronounced.

Vingt-<u>et</u>-un : vɛ̃-<u>t</u>e-ɛ̃
Vingt-<u>et</u>-une : vɛ̃-<u>t</u>e-yn
Vingt-deux : vɛ̃-<u>t</u>dø
Vingt-trois : vɛ̃-<u>t</u>tʁwa
Vingt-quatre : vɛ̃-<u>t</u>katʁ
etc.

Numbers from 70 to 99 are by far the most confusing for people learning French:

Number	Masculine	Feminine	Pronunciation (IPA)	
70	soixante-dix		swasɑ̃-tdis	
71	soixante-et-onze		swasɑ̃-te-ɔ̃z	
72	soixante-douze		swasɑ̃-tduz	
76	soixante-seize		swasɑ̃-tsɛz	
79	soixante-dix-neuf		swasɑ̃-tdi-**z**nœf	
80	quatre-vingts		katʁə-vɛ̃	
81	quatre-vingt-un	quatre-vingt-une	katʁə-vɛ̃-ɛ̃	katʁə-vɛ̃-yn
82	quatre-vingt-deux		katʁə-vɛ̃-dø	
90	quatre-vingt-dix		katʁə-vɛ̃-dis	
91	quatre-vingt-onze		katʁə-vɛ̃-ɔ̃z	
92	quatre-vingt-douze		katʁə-vɛ̃-duz	
97	quatre-vingt-dix-sept		katʁə-vɛ̃-di-sɛt	
99	quatre-vingt-dix-neuf		katʁə-vɛ̃-di-**z**nœf	

Let's try to understand how these three tens work, one by one.

De soixante-dix à soixante-dix-neuf (from 70 to 79)

Instead of inaugurating a new ten, this ten actually continues the count of the previous one (soixante):

68: *soixante-<u>h</u>uit* (sixty-**eight**)
69: *soixante-neuf* (sixty-**nine**)
70: *soixante-dix* (sixty-**ten**)

71: *soixante-et-onze* (sixty-and-**eleven**)
72: *soixante-douze* (sixty-**twelve**)
and so forth until
79: *soixante-dix-neuf* (sixty-**nineteen**)

De quatre-vingt à quatre-vingt-neuf (from 80 to 89)

Although intimidating at first sight, the word *quatre-vingts* («four twenties») shouldn't bother you too much. When counting or using numbers from this ten, French people don't even think of the actual, literal meaning of *quatre-vingts*. Just do the same, knowing that besides 81, the whole ten is perfectly regular. See for yourself:

80: *quatre-vingts*
81: *quatre-vingt-un(e)*
82: *quatre-vingt-deux*
83: *quatre-vingt-trois*
and so forth until
89: *quatre-vingt-neuf*

⚠ *Quatre-vingts* doesn't take an S when followed by another number.

⚠ Unlike other numbers ending with *un*, the number 81 doesn't use the word *et* (and).
81: *Quatre-vingt-un* (quatre-vingt-et-un).

Pronunciation

→ The final **E** in the number *quatre*, usually silent, is pronounced ə in numbers 80 to 89.
80: *katʁə-vɛ̃*
81: katʁə-vɛ̃-ɛ̃ / katʁə-vɛ̃-yn
82: katʁə-vɛ̃-dø
83: katʁə-vɛ̃-tʁwa
and so forth until
89: katʁə-vɛ̃-nœf

→ Letters **G**, **T** and **S** in the word *vingt(s)* are **always silent** in this ten: vɛ̃.

De quatre-vingt-dix à quatre-vingt-dix-neuf (from 90 to 99)

As with the numbers from 70 to 79, you just have to continue the count of the previous ten (quatre-vingts):

88: *quatre-vingt-huit* (eighty-**eight**)
89: *quatre-vingt-neuf* (eighty-**nine**)

90: *quatre-vingt-dix* (eighty-**ten**)
91: *quatre-vingt-onze* (eighty-**eleven**)
92: *quatre-vingt-douze* (eighty-**twelve**)
and so forth until
99: *quatre-vingt-dix-neuf* (eighty-**nineteen**)

⚠ Unlike 71 (*soixante-**et**-onze*), the number 91 doesn't use the word *et* (and).
91: *Quatre-vingt-onze* (quatre-vingt-et-onze).

→ The pronunciation rules for numbers 80 to 89 (*quatre* pronounced katʁə + silent letters G, T) apply equally to numbers 90 to 99.

→ A few French-speaking regions (notably Belgium and Switzerland) have specific words for the numbers 70, 80, 90: *septante, huitante, nonante*. Unfortunately, this much simpler and more logical system is not used in France nor most other French-speaking countries!

The following cardinal adjectives present no particular difficulty.

Number	Masculine	Feminine	Pronunciation (IPA)	
100	cent		sɑ̃	
101	cent-un	cent-une	sɑ̃-ɛ̃	sɑ̃-yn
102	cent-deux		sɑ̃-dø	
110	cent-dix		sɑ̃-dis	
111	cent-onze		sɑ̃-ɔ̃z	
116	cent-seize		sɑ̃-sɛz	
150	cent-cinquante		sɑ̃-sɛ̃kɑ̃t	
192	cent-quatre-vingt-douze		sɑ̃-katʁə-vɛ̃-duz	
200	deux-cents		dø-sɑ̃	
201	deux-cent-un	deux-cent-une	dø-sɑ̃-ɛ̃	dø-sɑ̃-yn
202	deux-cent-deux		dø-sɑ̃-dø	
215	deux-cent-quinze		dø-sɑ̃-kɛ̃z	
278	deux-cent-soixante-dix-huit		dø-sɑ̃-swasɑ̃-tdi-zɥit	
300	trois-cents		tʁwa-sɑ̃	
400	quatre-cents		katʁə-sɑ̃	
500	cinq-cents		sɛ̃-sɑ̃	
1000	mille		mil	
1001	mille-un	mille-une	mil-ɛ̃	mil-yn
1002	mille-deux		mil-dø	
1011	mille-onze		mil-ɔ̃z	
1978	mille-neuf-cent-soixante-dix-huit		mil-nœf-sɑ̃-swasɑ̃-tdi-zɥit	

2000	deux-mille	dø-mil
3000	trois-mille	tʁwa-mil
97 000	quatre-vingt-dix-sept-mille	katʁə-vɛ̃-di-sɛt-mil
100 000	cent-mille	sã-mil
200 000	deux-cent-mille	dø-sã-mil
1 000 000	un million	ɛ̃ miljɔ̃
2 000 000	deux millions	dø miljɔ̃
2 500 000	deux-millions-cinq-cent-mille	dø-miljɔ̃-sɛ̃-sã-mil
1 000 000 000	un milliard	ɛ̃ miljaʁ
2 500 000 000	deux-milliards-cinq-cent-millions	dø-miljaʁ-sɛ̃-sã-miljɔ̃

⚠ From one million upwards, cardinal adjectives are always followed by the word **de/d'**.

Neuf-cent-mille hommes.
*Un million **d'**hommes.*
Cinq-cent-mille femmes.
*Deux millions **de** femmes.*

Pronunciation

→ The final **Q** in the number *cinq* becomes silent when followed by another number.

105: sã-sɛ̃k
500: sɛ̃-sã
505: sɛ̃-sã-sɛ̃k
5000: sɛ̃-mil
5 000 000: sɛ̃ miljɔ̃ ; sɛ̃k miljɔ̃ is also accepted.
5 000 000 000: sɛ̃ miljaʁ ; sɛ̃k miljaʁ is also accepted.

→ The **final T** in the number *cent* is **always** silent when used in compound numbers.
101 : sã-ɛ̃ (sã-tɛ̃)

But the T (or S) is pronounced when followed by a noun.
cent hommes : sã **t**ɔm.
deux-cents hommes : dø-sã **z**ɔm.

Spelling

→ The word *cent* doesn't take an S when followed by another number.

200: *deux-cent**s***

201: *deux-cent-un*
300: *trois-cents*
350: *trois-cent-cinquante*
1500: *mille-cinq-cents*

⚠ This isn't the case of *millions* and *milliards*.

2 000 000: *deux-millions*
2 500 000 000: *deux-milliards-cinq-cent-millions*

→ The word thousand is completely **invariable**.

1000: *mille*
2000: *deux-mille*
2500: *deux-mille-cinq-cents*

⚠ French doesn't put any space, comma or period between thousands and hundreds.

Ordinal adjectives

If cardinal adjectives in French are utterly complicated, ordinal adjectives are strikingly simple!

Number	Masculine	Feminine	Pronunciation (IPA)	
1ᵉʳ	premier	première	pʁəmje	pʁəmjeʁ
2ⁿᵈ	second	seconde	səgɔ̃	səgɔ̃d
2ᵉᵐᵉ	deuxième		døzjɛm	
3ᵉᵐᵉ	troisième		tʁwazjɛm	
4ᵉᵐᵉ	quatrième		katʁijɛm	
5ᵉᵐᵉ	cinquième		sɛ̃kjɛm	
6ᵉᵐᵉ	sixième		sizjɛm	
9ᵉᵐᵉ	neuvième		nœvjɛm	
10ᵉᵐᵉ	dixième		dizjɛm	
11ᵉᵐᵉ	onzième		ɔ̃zjɛm	
19ᵉᵐᵉ	dix-neuvième		di-znœvjɛm	
50ᵉᵐᵉ	cinquantième		sɛ̃kɑ̃tjɛm	
70ᵉᵐᵉ	soixante-dixième		swasɑ̃-tdizjɛm	
80ᵉᵐᵉ	quatre-vingtième		katʁə-vɛ̃tjɛm	
98ᵉᵐᵉ	quatre-vingt-dix-huitième		katʁə-vɛ̃-di-zɥitjɛm	
100ᵉᵐᵉ	centième		sɑ̃tjɛm	
101ᵉᵐᵉ	cent-unième		sɑ̃-ynjɛm	

102ème	cent-deuxième		sã-døzjɛm	
500ème	cinq-centième		sɛ̃-sãtjɛm	
1000ème	millième		miljɛm	
1001ème	mille-et-unième		mi-le-ynjɛm	
1046ème	mille-quarante-sixième		mil-kaʁã-tsizjɛm	
10 000ème	dix-millième		di-miljɛm	
75 000ème	soixante-quinze-millième		swasã-tkɛ̃z-miljɛm	
100 000ème	cent-millième		sã-miljɛm	
500 000ème	cinq-cent-millième		sɛ̃-sã-miljɛm	
1 000 000ème	millionième		miljɔnjɛm	
1 000 000 000 ème	milliardième		miljaʁdjɛm	
second to last	avant-dernier	avant-dernière	avã-dɛʁnje	avã-dɛʁnjɛʁ
last	dernier	dernière	dɛʁnje	dɛʁnjɛʁ

→ As you can see, to form ordinal adjectives in French, you just have to add the suffix **-ième** to the cardinal adjective. Some numbers require minor spelling adjustments:

Deux > deuxième (døzjɛm)
Trois > troisième
Quatre > quatrième
Cinq > cinquième
Neuf > neuvième
etc.

Exceptions to this rule are rare:

→ The word *premier/première* is the French equivalent of the English word «*first*».

→ The word *second/seconde* is usually used when the designated noun is both **second and last**.
Ex: *La Seconde Guerre mondiale* (the Second World War), for there is no Third World War.
But: *Le deuxième pays le plus grand du monde* (the second biggest country in the world).

→ Millionth is *millionième*, not *un millionième*.
Billionth is *milliardième*, not *un milliardième*.

Pronunciation

→ As mentioned in Chapter 1.1, the word second/seconde is pronounced səgɔ̃/səgɔ̃d.

→ The X in *deuxième*, *sixième* and *dixième* is pronounced **Z**: døzjɛm, sizjɛm, dizjɛm.

→ The T in *cent* is **always** silent in compound numbers, even when followed by a vowel.

Cent-unième : sã-ynjɛm (sã-tynjɛm)

→ The usual rules of liaisons apply.

Mon premier amour (my first love) : mɔ̃ pʁəmje ʁamuʁ

Exercises

1. Fill in the blanks to form the feminine form of the following words.

*   violent > viol____
*   gentil > gent___
*   poli > pol__
*   beau > be___
*   agréable > agréab__
*   passif > pass___
*   vieux > vi____
*   artificiel > artific____
*   étranger > étrang___
*   secret > secr___
*   menteur > ment____

2. Which of the following sentences are incorrect? Explain why.

*   Les chevaux noirs
*   Un cheval et une jument brunes
*   D'aimables femmes
*   Les gentilles acteurs
*   Un américain homme
*   La blanche colombe (in poetic context)
*   Un nouveau ami
*   De la bonne musique

3. Link the following demonstrative adjectives with the appropriate nouns.

Ce	maisons
Cette	homme
Ces	amie
Cet	éléphant
Cette	huîtres

Ces   héros
Cet   femme

4. Fill in the blanks with the appropriate indefinite adjective.

ex: *He loves another woman* > Il aime une <u>autre</u> femme.

Dresses of various colors > Des robes de _____ couleurs.

He's had a few drinks > Il a bu _____ verres.

No man is an island > ___ homme n'est une île.

She went bankrupt several times > Elle a fait faillite _____ fois.

They are the same age > Ils ont le _____ âge.

All taxes included > _____ taxes comprises.

Some men are violent > _____ hommes sont violents.

5. Correct the following incorrect possessive adjectives.

ex: *Her car is yellow* > Son voiture est jaune (Sa).

I saw his parents yesterday > J'ai vu son parents hier.

She repairs her bike > Elle répare sa vélo.

I love your eyes, darling > J'aime ses yeux, chérie.

That's their problem > C'est leurs problème.

Sarah is her friend > Sarah est sa amie.

This is our children's room > C'est la chambre de vos enfants.

Where's your car, guys? > Où est ta voiture, les gars ?

6. Tick the sentences where the S of *quels/quelles* is pronounced.

- Quels artistes aimez-vous ? *(Which artists do you like?)* ☐
- Quels héros ! *(What heroes!)* ☐
- Quelles héroïnes t'inspire ? *(Which heroines inspire you?)* ☐
- Quelles idiotes ! *(What idiots!)* ☐

- Quels habits choisir ? *(What clothes to choose?)* ☐
- Quelles harpes as-tu achetées ? *(What harps have you bought?)* ☐
- Quels beaux chevaux ! *(What beautiful horses!)* ☐

7. Write the following cardinal numbers in words.

1 amie > _____ amie.

11 chanteuses > _____ chanteuses.

19 hommes > _____ hommes.

44 îles > _____ îles.

72 chiens > _____ chiens.

81 femmes > _____ femmes.

499 musiciens > _____ musiciens.

l'année 2024 > l'année _____.

350 000 euros > _____ euros.

8 000 000 000 d'habitants > _____ d'habitants.

8. Translate the following sentences in English.

La première maison >

La deuxième symphonie >

La seconde épouse >

La onzième fille >

La dix-septième heure >

La quatre-vingt-treizième voiture >

Le cent-unième dalmatien >

L'avant-dernière fois >

Le dernier empereur >

4. Basic Vocabulary

N ow that you've mastered the French nominal system, it's time to take a well-deserved break with a little vocabulary. In this chapter, you'll discover many of the words and expressions used by the French in everyday life. Are you ready?

4.1 Greetings & Everyday expressions

Greetings & Expressions	Pronunciation (IPA)	Meaning
Bonjour	bɔ̃ʒuʁ	Good morning, Hello
Salut	saly	Hi
Coucou	kuku	Hey there!
Allô ?	alo ?	Hello? (on the phone)
Bonsoir	bɔ̃swaʁ	Good evening
Bonne nuit !	bɔn nɥi	Good night!
Bienvenue	bjɛ̃vny	Welcome
Comment ça va ?	kɔmɑ̃ sa va ?	How are you?
Ça va ?	sa va ?	
Comment allez-vous ?	kɔmɑ̃ tale vu ?	How are you? (formal or plural)
Ça va.	sa va.	I'm fine
Quoi de neuf ?	kwa dnœf ?	What's up?
Enchanté(e)	ɑ̃ʃɑ̃te	Nice to meet you
Comment vous appelez-vous ?	kɔmɑ̃ vu zaple vu ?	What's your name? (formal or plural)
Comment tu t'appelles ?	kɔmɑ̃ ty tapɛl ?	What's your name? (informal)
À plus tard	a ply taʁ	See you later
À tout à l'heure	a tu ta lœʁ	
À bientôt	a bjɛ̃to	See you again
Au revoir	o ʁəvwaʁ	Goodbye
Excusez-moi	ɛkskyze mwa	Excuse me
Je vous demande pardon	ʒə vu dəmɑ̃d paʁdɔ̃	I beg your pardon (formal)
S'il vous plaît	sil vu plɛ	Please
Merci	mɛʁsi	Thank you
Merci beaucoup	mɛʁsi boku	Thank you very much

→ Have you noticed the liaisons in some of the expressions above?

Important: In French, exclamation marks, question marks, colons and semicolons are always preceded by a space. This typographical rule is called "French spacing".

4.2 People & Professions

M/F	People & Professions	Pronunciation (IPA)	Meaning
un	homme	ɔm	a man
une	femme	fam	a woman
une	personne	pɛʁsɔn	a person
un	garçon	gaʁsɔ̃	a boy
une	fille	fij	a girl
un, une	enfant	ɑ̃fɑ̃	a child
un	bébé	bebe	a baby
un, une	jeune	ʒœn	a youngster
un, une	adulte	adylt	an adult
une	personne âgée	pɛʁsɔn aʒe	an elderly person
adjective	jeune	ʒœn	young
adjective	vieux, vieille	vjø, vjɛj	old
un	père	pɛʁ	a father
une	mère	mɛʁ	a mother
une	fille	fij	a daughter
un	fils	fis	a son
une	sœur	sœʁ	a sister
un	frère	fʁɛʁ	a brother
un	oncle	ɔ̃kl	an uncle
une	tante	tɑ̃t	an aunt
un, une	neveu, nièce	nəvø, njɛs	a nephew, a niece
un, une	cousin, cousine	kuzɛ̃, kuzin	a cousin
un	grand-père	gʁɑ̃pɛʁ	a grandfather
une	grand-mère	gʁɑ̃mɛʁ	a grandmother
un, une	petit-fils, petite-fille	pətifis, pətitfij	a grandson, a granddaughter
des	petits-enfants	pətizɑ̃fɑ̃	grandchildren
une	famille	famij	a family
un	métier	metje	a job, a trade, a profession
un	travail	tʁavaj	a job, a trade, a profession
une	profession	pʁɔfesjɔ̃	a job, a trade, a profession
un	boulot	bulo	a job (informal)
le	travail	tʁavaj	work
un, une	travailleur, travailleuse	tʁavajœʁ, tʁavajøz	a worker

un, une	élève	elɛv	a pupil, a student
un, une	étudiant, étudiante	etydjɑ̃, etydjɑ̃t	a student
un, une	retraité, retraitée	ʁətʁete	a pensioner
un, une	salarié, salariée	salaʁje	an employee
un, une	employé, employée	ɑ̃plwaje	
un, une	boulanger, boulangère	bulɑ̃ʒe, bulɑ̃ʒeʁ	a baker
un, une	policier, policière	pɔlisje, pɔlisjeʁ	a police officer
un, une	pompier, pompière	pɔ̃pje, pɔ̃pjeʁ	a firefighter
un, une	docteur, docteure	dɔktœʁ	
un, une	médecin, femme médecin	medsɛ̃, fam medsɛ̃	a physician
la	médecine	medsin	medicine (the discipline)
un, une	instituteur, institutrice	ɛ̃stitytœʁ, ɛ̃stitytʁis	a primary school teacher
un, une	enseignant, enseignante	ɑ̃sɛɲɑ̃, ɑ̃sɛɲɑ̃t	a teacher
un, une	professeur, professeure	pʁɔfesœʁ	
un, une	garagiste	gaʁaʒist	a mechanic
un, une	infirmier, infirmière	ɛ̃fiʁmje, ɛ̃fiʁmjeʁ	a nurse
un, une	boucher, bouchère	buʃe, buʃeʁ	a butcher
un, une	coiffeur, coiffeuse	kwafœʁ, kwaføz	a hairdresser
un, une	facteur, factrice	faktœʁ, faktʁis	a postman, a postwoman
un, une	serveur, serveuse	sɛʁvœʁ, sɛʁvøz	a waiter, a waitress

4.3 Places & Directions

M/F	Places & Directions	Pronunciation (IPA)	Meaning
une	ville	vil	a town, a city
un	village	vilaʒ	a village
une	banlieue	bɑ̃ljø	a suburb
un	pays	pei	a country
une	gare	gaʁ	a train station
une	gare routière	gaʁ ʁutjeʁ	a bus station
un	arrêt de bus	aʁɛ də bys	a bus stop
un	parking	paʁkiŋ	a parking lot
une	route	ʁut	a road

une	autoroute	otoʁut	a highway
une	rue	ʁy	a street
une	place	plas	a square
un	rond-point	ʁɔ̃pwɛ̃	a roundabout
un	passage piéton	pasaʒ pjetɔ̃	a crosswalk
un	feu rouge	fø ʁuʒ	a traffic light
le	centre-ville	sɑ̃tʁəvil	downtown
une	maison	mɛzɔ̃	a house
un	bâtiment	batimɑ̃	a building
un	immeuble	imœbl	
une	banque	bɑ̃k	a bank
une	mairie	meʁi	a city hall
un	commissariat	kɔmisaʁja	a police station
une	gendarmerie	ʒɑ̃daʁməʁi	
une	caserne de pompiers	kazɛʁn də pɔ̃pje	a fire station
un	magasin	magazɛ̃	a shop
une	boutique	butik	
un	restaurant	ʁɛstɔʁɑ̃	a restaurant
une	église	egliz	a church
une	cathédrale	katedʁal	a cathedral
une	tour	tuʁ	a tower
une	bibliothèque	biblijɔtɛk	a library
un	musée	myze	a museum
un	château	ʃato	a castle
un	square	skwaʁ	a park,
un	parc	paʁk	a public garden
un	pont	pɔ̃	a bridge
un	marché	maʁʃe	a market
un	supermarché	sypɛʁmaʁʃe	a supermarket
le	nord	nɔʁ	North
le	sud	syd	South
l'	est	ɛst	East
l'	ouest	wɛst	West
	à gauche	a goʃ	to the left
	à droite	a dʁwat	to the right
	tout droit	tu dʁwa	straight ahead

	devant	dəvã	in front of
	en face de	ã fas də	
	au milieu de	o miljø də	in the middle of
	derrière	dɛʁjɛʁ	behind
	près de	pʁɛ də	close to
	à côté de	a kote də	
	Où est… ?	u ɛ… ?	Where is… ?

4.4 Meals & Food

M/F	Meals & Food	Pronunciation (IPA)	Meaning
le	petit déjeuner	pəti deʒœne	breakfast
le	déjeuner	deʒœne	lunch
le	goûter	gute	after-school snack
le	dîner	dine	dinner
un	plat	pla	a dish
un	repas	ʁəpa	a meal
une	assiette	asjɛt	a plate
une	fourchette	fuʁʃɛt	a fork
un	couteau	kuto	a knife
une	cuillère	kɥijɛʁ	a spoon
des	couverts	kuvɛʁ	cutlery
un	verre	vɛʁ	a glass
la	nourriture	nuʁityʁ	food
la	cuisine	kɥizin	the kitchen, cooking
un	apéritif	apeʁitif	an aperitif
une	entrée	ãtʁe	a starter
le	plat principal	pla pʁɛ̃sipal	the main course
une	salade	salad	a salad
du	fromage	fʁɔmaʒ	cheese
un	dessert	desɛʁ	a dessert
un	bonbon	bɔ̃bɔ̃	a candy
un	gâteau	gato	a cake
du	pain	pɛ̃	bread
du	sel	sɛl	salt
du	poivre	pwavʁ	pepper
de la	moutarde	mutaʁd	mustard

de l'	huile	ɥil	oil
un, des	œuf, œufs	œf, ə	an egg
des	pâtes	pat	pasta
du	riz	ʁi	rice
du	sucre	sykʁ	sugar
de la	confiture	kɔ̃fityʁ	jam, marmalade
un	fruit	fʁɥi	a fruit
une	pomme	pɔm	an apple
une	poire	pwaʁ	a pear
une	fraise	fʁɛz	a strawberry
une	framboise	fʁɑ̃bwaz	a raspberry
une	orange	ɔʁɑ̃ʒ	an orange
un	citron	sitʁɔ̃	a lemon
un	citron vert	sitʁɔ̃ vɛʁ	a lime
une	mandarine	mɑ̃daʁin	a tangerine
une	pêche	pɛʃ	a peach
un	abricot	abʁiko	an apricot
une	prune	pʁyn	a plum
une	cerise	səʁiz	a cherry
une	noix	nwa	a walnut
une	cacahuète	kakawɛt	a peanut
un	ananas	ananas	a pineapple
du	raisin	ʁɛzɛ̃	grape
un	légume	legym	a vegetable
une	pomme de terre	pɔm də tɛʁ	a potato
une	patate	patat	
une	carotte	kaʁɔt	a carrot
un	champignon	ʃɑ̃piɲɔ̃	a mushroom
un	haricot	aʁiko	a bean
un	haricot vert	aʁiko vɛʁ	a green bean
un	oignon	ɔɲɔ̃	an onion
du	maïs	mais	corn
un	petit pois	pəti pwa	a pea
un	chou	ʃu	a cabbage
un	chou-fleur	ʃu flœʁ	a cauliflower
des (masc.)	épinards	epinaʁ	spinach

une	tomate	tɔmat	a tomato
un	poivron	pwavʁɔ̃	a bell pepper
un	poireau	pwaʁo	a leak
du	beurre	bœʁ	butter
du	lait	lɛ	milk
de la	crème	kʁɛm	cream
de la	glace	glas	ice, ice cream
un, du	yaourt	jauʁt	yogurt
de la	viande	vjɑ̃d	meat
du	jambon	ʒɑ̃bɔ̃	ham
du	porc	pɔʁ	pork
du	poulet	pulɛ	chicken
du	poisson	pwasɔ̃	fish
une	saucisse	sosis	a sausage
du	veau	vo	veal

4.5 Clothing & Accessories

M/F	Clothing & Accessories	Pronunciation (IPA)	Meaning
un	vêtement	vɛtmɑ̃	a clothing item
des	vêtements	vɛtmɑ̃	clothes
un	chapeau	ʃapo	a hat
une	casquette	kaskɛt	a cap
un	bonnet	bɔnɛ	a beanie
des (fem.)	lunettes	lynɛt	glasses
des (fem.)	boucles d'oreilles	bukl dɔʁɛj	earrings
une	écharpe	eʃaʁp	a scarf
un	t-shirt	tiʃœʁt	a t-shirt
un	maillot	majo	an undershirt
une	chemise	ʃəmiz	a shirt
un	pull-over	pylɔvɛʁ	a pullover
une	veste	vɛst	a jacket
un	manteau	mɑ̃to	a coat
une	ceinture	sɛ̃tyʁ	a belt
un	pantalon	pɑ̃talɔ̃	trousers
une	robe	ʁɔb	a dress
une	jupe	ʒyp	a skirt

des (fem.)	chaussettes	ʃosɛt	socks
des (fem.)	chaussures	ʃosyʁ	shoes
des (fem.)	bottes	bɔt	boots
des (fem.)	tongs	tɔ̃g	flip-flops
une	bague	bag	a ring

4.6 Body

M/F	Body	Pronunciation (IPA)	Meaning
un	corps	kɔʁ	a body
une	partie du corps	paʁti dy kɔʁ	a body part
la	tête	tɛt	the head
un, des	cheveu, cheveux	ʃəvə	hair (on the head)
un, des	poil, poils	pwal	hair (elsewhere)
le	visage	vizaʒ	the face
le	front	fʁɔ̃	the forehead
un, des	œil, yeux	œj, jə	an eye, the eyes
un	sourcil	suʁsil	an eyebrow
un	cil	sil	an eyelash
une	joue	ʒu	a cheek
la	bouche	buʃ	the mouth
le	menton	mɑ̃tɔ̃	the chin
une	oreille	ɔʁɛj	an ear
une	dent	dɑ̃	a tooth
la	langue	lɑ̃g	the tongue
les (fem.)	lèvres	lɛvʁ	the lips
le	cou	ku	the neck
une	épaule	epol	a shoulder
le	dos	do	the back
la	poitrine	pwatʁin	the chest
les (masc.)	seins	sɛ̃	breasts
le	ventre	vɑ̃tʁ	the stomach
un	bras	bʁa	an arm
un	coude	kud	an elbow
un	poignet	pwaɲɛ	a wrist
une	main	mɛ̃	a hand
un	doigt	dwa	a finger

un	ongle	ɔ̃gl	a nail
le	pouce	pus	the thumb
le	bassin	basɛ̃	the pelvis
une	hanche	ɑ̃ʃ	a hip
une	jambe	ʒɑ̃b	a leg
une	cuisse	kɥis	a thigh
les (fem.)	fesses	fɛs	the buttocks
un	genou	ʒənu	a knee
une	cheville	ʃəvij	an ankle
un	pied	pje	a foot
un	talon	talɔ̃	a heel
un	orteil	ɔʁtɛj	a toe

4.7 Nature & Weather

M/F	Nature & Weather	Pronunciation (IPA)	Meaning
le	jour	ʒuʁ	day
la	nuit	nɥi	night
le	printemps	pʁɛ̃tɑ̃	spring
l' (masc.)	été	ete	summer
l' (masc.)	automne	otɔn	fall
l' (masc.)	hiver	ivɛʁ	winter
le	soleil	sɔlɛj	the sun
la	lune	lyn	the moon
le	monde	mɔ̃d	the world
le	ciel	sjɛl	the sky
un	nuage	nɥaʒ	a cloud
la	pluie	plɥi	the rain
la	neige	nɛʒ	the snow
la	tempête	tɑ̃pɛt	the storm
le	temps	tɑ̃	weather, time
la	nature	natyʁ	nature
un	animal	animal	an animal
un, une	chien, chienne	ʃjɛ̃, ʃjɛn	a dog
un, une	chat, chatte	ʃa, ʃat	a cat
un	oiseau	wazo	a bird
une	vache	vaʃ	a cow

un	insecte	ɛ̃sɛkt	an insect
une	plante	plɑ̃t	a plant
une	forêt	fɔʁɛ	a forest

4.8 Days & Months

M/F	Days & Months	Pronunciation (IPA)	Meaning
(le)	lundi	lœ̃di	Monday
	mardi	maʁdi	Tuesday
	mercredi	mɛʁkʁədi	Wednesday
	jeudi	ʒødi	Thursday
	vendredi	vɑ̃dʁədi	Friday
	samedi	samdi	Saturday
	dimanche	dimɑ̃ʃ	Sunday
un	jour	ʒuʁ	day
une	semaine	səmɛn	a week
	janvier	ʒɑ̃vje	January
	février	fevʁije	February
	mars	maʁs	March
	avril	avʁil	April
	mai	mɛ	May
	juin	ʒɥɛ̃	June
	juillet	ʒɥijɛ	July
	août	ut	August
	septembre	sɛptɑ̃bʁ	September
	octobre	ɔktɔbʁ	October
	novembre	nɔvɑ̃bʁ	November
	décembre	desɑ̃bʁ	December
un	mois	mwa	a month
un	an	ɑ̃	a year
une	année	ane	

4.9 Colors & Adjectives

Colors & Adjectives (m,f)	Pronunciation (IPA)	Meaning
blanc, blanche	blɑ̃, blɑ̃ʃ	white
noir, noire	nwaʁ	black

gris, grise	gʁi, gʁiz	grey
rouge	ʁuʒ	red
jaune	ʒon	yellow
vert, verte	vɛʁ, vɛʁt	green
bleu, bleue	blø	blue
bleu marine	blø maʁin	navy blue
bleu ciel	blø sjɛl	sky-blue
rose	ʁoz	pink
orange	ɔʁɑ̃ʒ	orange
marron	maʁɔ̃	brown
brun, brune	bʁœ̃, bʁyn	brown
violet, violette	vjɔlɛ, vjɔlɛt	purple
mauve	mov	mauve
bordeaux	bɔʁdo	burgundy
doré, dorée	dɔʁe	gold
argenté, argentée	aʁʒɑ̃te	silver
bon, bonne	bɔ̃, bɔn	good
bien	bjɛ̃	well
beau, belle	bo, bɛl	beautiful
mauvais, mauvaise	movɛ, movɛz	bad
moche	mɔʃ	ugly
laid, laide	lɛ, lɛd	ugly
grand, grande	gʁɑ̃, gʁɑ̃d	tall, big
large	laʁʒ	wide, large
gros, grosse	gʁo, gʁos	big, fat
mince	mɛ̃s	thin
petit, petite	pəti, pətit	small, little
fort, forte	fɔʁ, fɔʁt	strong
faible	fɛbl	weak
solide	sɔlid	solid
fragile	fʁaʒil	fragile
léger, légère	leʒe, leʒɛʁ	light
seul, seule	sœl	alone
libre	libʁ	free
chaud, chaude	ʃo	warm, hot
froid, froide	fʁwa, fʁwad	cold
nouveau, nouvelle	nuvo, nuvɛl	new

ancien, ancienne	ãsjɛ̃, ãsjɛn	old, former
riche	ʁiʃ	rich
pauvre	povʁ	poor
simple	sɛ̃pl	simple
facile	fasil	easy
difficile	difisil	difficult
dur, dure	dyʁ	hard
compliqué	kɔ̃plike	complicated
rapide	ʁapid	fast
lent, lente	lã, lãt	slow
heureux, heureuse	œʁø, œʁøz	happy
malheureux, malheureuse	malœʁø, malœʁøz	unhappy
triste	tʁist	sad
sympathique	sɛ̃patik	nice, friendly
sympa	sɛ̃pa	
gentil, gentille	ʒãti, ʒãtij	kind, nice
méchant, méchante	meʃã, meʃãt	mean, evil
propre	pʁɔpʁ	clean
sale	sal	dirty
public, publique	pyblik	public
privé, privée	pʁive	private
intéressant, intéressante	ɛ̃teʁesã, ɛ̃teʁesãt	interesting
ennuyeux	ãnɥijø, ãnɥijøz	boring
dangereux, dangereuse	dãʒʁø, dãʒʁøz	dangerous
amusant, amusante	amyzã, amyzãt	funny
drôle	dʁol	
génial, géniale	ʒenjal	great, awesome
super	sypɛʁ	
formidable	fɔʁmidabl	
passionnant	pasjɔnã	fascinating
calme	kalm	calm,quiet
tranquille	tʁãkil	
timide	timid	shy
effrayant, effrayante	efʁɛjã, efʁɛjãt	scary
cher, chère	ʃɛʁ	expensive
courageux, courageuse	kuʁaʒø, kuʁaʒøz	brave
fatigué, fatiguée	fatige	tired

grave	ɡʁav	serious
sérieux, sérieuse	seʁjø, seʁjøz	
inquiet, inquiète	ɛ̃kjɛ, ɛ̃kjɛt	worried
doux, douce	du, dus	soft
intelligent, intelligente	ɛ̃teliʒɑ̃, ɛ̃teliʒɑ̃t	intelligent
malin, maligne	malɛ̃, maliɲ	smart, clever
bête	bɛt	stupid
idiot, idiote	idjo, idjɔt	
stupide	stypid	
utile	ytil	useful
précédent, précédente	pʁesedɑ̃, pʁesedɑ̃t	previous
suivant, suivante	sɥivɑ̃, sɥivɑ̃t	next
vrai, vraie	vʁɛ	true
faux, fausse	fo, fos	false

Exercise

Translate the following English sentences into French.

1. *Hello, how are you?*

_____ , _____ ?

2. *Nice to meet you. I'm fine, thank you.*

_____. _____ , _____.

3. *A young girl and her nephew.*

_____ et _____.

4. *A nurse and two policewomen.*

_____ et _____.

5. *Grey hair, blue eyes and pink toes.*

_____ , _____ et _____.

6. *Scary clouds and a strong rain.*

_____ et _____ .

7. *The third Sunday of December.*

_____ de _____ .

8. *Some big, dangerous dogs.*

_____ .

9. *Where is the library, please?*

_____ , _____ ?

10. *A white and gold skirt.*

_____ et _____ .

5. Present indicative (part 1)

t's time to get to grips with the French verbal system. Let's face it: it's infinitely more complicated than its English equivalent. But, as is often the case, it follows a certain logic, and exceptions are rare. In fact, 90% of French verbs are conjugated in the same way! Let's dig into it.

5.1 Personal pronouns

As in English, French verbs in the indicative mood are usually preceded by a personal pronoun. As you can see, French personal pronouns are very similar to their English counterparts, with a few noticeable differences:

French pronouns	English translation
Je, J'	I
Tu	You (singular)
Il/Elle/On	He/She/We (informal)
Nous	We (formal)
Vous	You (plural)
Ils/Elles	They (masculine/feminine)

→ The first-person singular *Je* becomes *J'* before a vowel or a silent H.

Je mange (I eat)
Je hais (I hate)
J'adore (I adore)
J'hésite (I hesitate)

→ Like most other Romance languages (or like Old English *Thou/Ye*), French uses a different pronoun for the second person singular and the second person plural. *Vous* (the plural "you") is also used when addressing someone you don't know, or towards whom you wish to show a particular form of respect: an elderly person, a priest, your boss, etc.

⚠ Adjectives agree in gender and number, not according to personal pronouns.

Example: *You are nice.*

(2nd person singular, to a friend, a child, a relative): *Tu es gentil(le)*
(2nd person plural, to a group of people): *Vous êtes gentil(le)s*
(2nd person plural, to a stranger, or a figure of authority): *Vous êtes gentil(le)*

→ The French have two ways of saying "we". In everyday life and informal language, French people tend to use the pronoun *On* (conjugated as the third person singular). In more formal speech, they use the actual first person singular, *Nous*, with the appropriate conjugation. The meaning of the sentence remains the same in both cases.

Example: *We always eat early.*

(informal): ***On*** *mange toujours tôt.*
(formal): ***Nous*** *mangeons toujours tôt.*

→ As in English (*he/she*), the French language uses gendered pronouns in the third person singular: ***Il, Elle***. As we'll soon see, this has no effect on conjugation, but you will of course need to agree adjectives accordingly.

He is smart > ***Il*** *est intelligent.*
She is smart > ***Elle*** *est intelligente.*

→ Although French doesn't have a third-person neutral personal pronoun like the English *it*, French people often use the construction *C'est* (*ce* + *est* = "*this is*") or the demonstrative pronoun *Ça* (*it, that*) to designate an impersonal reality or an object.

It's beautiful > ***C'est*** *beau.*
It smells bad, here > ***Ça*** *sent mauvais, ici.*

→ Unlike the English *they*, the third person plural also has a pronoun for each gender. These are very easy to memorize: they're the same as in the third person singular, but with a final S!

They (a group of men) are happy > ***Ils*** *sont heureux.*
They (a group of women) are happy > ***Elles*** *sont heureuses.*

5.2 First-group verbs

French verbs can be divided into three groups:

* First-group verbs: regular verbs whose **infinitive** ends in **-er**
* Second-group verbs: regular verbs whose **infinitive** ends in **-ir**
* Third-group verbs, including all **irregular** verbs

⚠ Most verbs ending in -er and -ir are regular verbs, belonging to the first and second group, respectively. However, a verb can end in -er and -ir and have irregular endings. In such case, this verb will automatically fall into the third group category.

The good news is that the vast majority of French verbs (over 90%) belong to the first group and are perfectly regular! So, all you have to do is memorize the first-group endings to conjugate almost all French verbs.

Now, let's get down to business.

How do you conjugate a verb in French?

The main difficulty with French conjugation lies in its endings, for the form of the conjugated verb changes according to the subject. This is also the case (to a lesser extent) in English, where the third person singular takes an S: *I want, He/she wants*.

Let's discover the first-group endings in French, for the *présent de l'indicatif* (present indicative).

PRESENT INDICATIVE / First-group endings	
Infinitive: *Chanter (ʃɑ̃te)*	English translation
Je chant**e**	I sing
Tu chant**es**	You sing (informal, singular)
Il/Elle chant**e**, On chant**e**	He/She sings, We sing (informal)
Nous chant**ons**	We sing (formal)
Vous chant**ez**	You sing (plural <u>or</u> formal singular)
Ils/Elles chant**ent**	They (m/f) sing

Have you noticed the endings?
-e / **-es** / **-e** / **-ons** / **-ez** / **-ent**
silent / silent / silent / ɔ̃ / e / silent

Let's see if they work with another first-group verb!

PRESENT INDICATIVE / First-group endings	
Infinitive: *Manger (Mɑ̃ʒe)*	English translation
Je mang**e**	I eat
Tu mang**es**	You eat (informal, singular)
Il/Elle mang**e**, On mang**e**	He/She eats, We eat (informal)
Nous mange**ons**	We eat (formal)
Vous mang**ez**	You eat (plural or formal singular)
Ils/Elles mang**ent**	They (m/f) eat

Congrats! Now, you know how to conjugate first-group verbs in the **present indicative** tense. As in English, this tense is used to designate an **action in progress**, a **recurring action** or to state a **general truth** about a person, an animal or a thing.

Examples:

Je mange un sandwich (an action in progress)
Le lundi, je mange au restaurant (a recurring action, a habit)
Je ne mange pas de viande (a general truth about someone/something)

Vocabulary

To help you get off to a good start in the world of French conjugation, here's a list of fifty commonly used first-group verbs in French. Once again, the conjugation of these verbs is perfectly regular in the present indicative (and usually in the other moods and tenses as well).

COMMON FIRST-GROUP VERBS		
Infinitive	Pronunciation (IPA)	Meaning
accepter	aksɛpte	to accept
acheter	aʃəte	to buy
adorer	adɔʁe	to adore
aider	ɛde	to help
aimer	ɛme	to love
appeler	aple	to call
apporter	apɔʁte	to bring
arriver	aʁive	to arrive
chercher	ʃɛʁʃe	to search
commencer	kɔmɑ̃se	to begin
danser	dɑ̃se	to dance
déjeuner	deʒœne	to have lunch
demander	dəmɑ̃de	to ask
démarrer	demaʁe	to start
détester	detɛste	to hate
discuter	diskyte	to discuss
donner	dɔne	to give
écouter	ekute	to listen
entrer	ɑ̃tʁe	to enter
envoyer	ɑ̃vwaje	to send
espérer	ɛspeʁe	to hope
étudier	etydje	to study
fermer	fɛʁme	to close, to shut
gagner	gaɲe	to win
garder	gaʁde	to keep
habiter	abitɛ	to dwell
inviter	ɛ̃vite	to invite
jeter	ʒəte	to throw
jouer	ʒwe	to play
laver	lave	to wash

marcher	maʁʃe	to walk
montrer	mɔ̃tʁe	to show
nager	naʒe	to swim
nettoyer	nɛtwaje	to clean
organiser	ɔʁganize	to organize
oublier	ublje	to forget
parler	paʁle	to speak, to talk
payer	peje	to pay
penser	pɑ̃se	to think
peser	pəze	to weigh
poser	poze	to put, to place
préférer	pʁefeʁe	to prefer
préparer	pʁepaʁe	to prepare
refuser	ʁəfyze	to refuse
regarder	ʁəgaʁde	to watch, to look at
rencontrer	ʁɑ̃kɔ̃tʁe	to meet
rester	ʁɛste	to stay, to remain
rêver	ʁɛve	to dream
tomber	tɔ̃be	to fall
travailler	tʁavaje	to work
trouver	tʁuve	to find
visiter	vizite	to visit
voler	vɔle	to fly or to steal
voyager	vwajaʒe	to travel

→ When an **e** (pronounced ə) is present in the last syllable of the root of an infinitive (ex: p<u>e</u>ser, ach<u>e</u>ter), it becomes **è** in the present indicative.

Peser *pəze* > *je p**è**se (pɛz), tu p**è**ses (pɛz), etc.*
Acheter *aʃəte* > *j'ach**è**te (aʃɛt), tu ach**è**tes (aʃɛt), etc.*

→ The final consonant of many **-eler/-eter verbs** is doubled. Pronunciation is thus modified.

Appeler *apəle* > *j'appe<u>ll</u>e (apɛl), tu appe<u>ll</u>es (apɛl), etc.*
Jeter *ʒəte* > *je je<u>tt</u>e (ʒɛt), tu je<u>tt</u>es (ʒɛt), etc.*

Notable exceptions: acheter, geler, modeler…

→ The **y** in -yer verbs becomes an **i**, except in the 1st and 2nd person plural.

Payer > *je paie, tu paies, il/elle/on paie, nous payons, vous payez, ils paient.*
Nettoyer > *je nettoie, tu nettoies, il/elle/on nettoie, nous nettoyons, vous nettoyez, ils nettoient.*
Envoyer > *j'envoie, tu envoies, il/elle/on envoie, nous envoyons, vous envoyez, ils envoient.*

5.3 Second-group verbs

Now that you've mastered the verbal system, let's find out how to conjugate second-group verbs in the present indicative tense. As you'll see, second-group verbs use a different set of endings to first-group verbs. They are, however, regular verbs, which means that these endings apply to all verbs in the second group, without exception.

Here are the second-group endings in the present indicative:

PRESENT INDICATIVE / Second-group endings	
Infinitive: *Choisir (ʃwaziʁ)*	English translation
Je chois**is**	I choose
Tu chois**is**	You choose (informal, singular)
Il/Elle chois**it**, On chois**it**	He/She chooses, We choose (informal)
Nous chois**issons**	We choose (formal)
Vous chois**issez**	You choose (plural <u>or</u> formal singular)
Ils/Elles chois**issent**	They (m/f) choose

-is / -is / -it / -issons / -issez / -issent
i / i / i / isɔ̃ / ise / is

Vocabulary

There are far fewer second-group verbs than first-group verbs, but these are still very common. Here are thirty common second-group verbs to get you started on the right foot.

COMMON SECOND-GROUP VERBS		
Infinitive	Pronunciation (IPA)	Meaning
accomplir	akɔ̃pliʁ	to accomplish
accueillir	akœjiʁ	to welcome
agir	aʒiʁ	to act
applaudir	aplodiʁ	to applaud
atterrir	ateʁiʁ	to land
avertir	avɛʁtiʁ	to warn
bénir	beniʁ	to bless

convertir	kɔ̃vɛʁtiʁ	to convert
définir	definiʁ	to define
envahir	ãvaiʁ	to invade
établir	etabliʁ	to establish
finir	finiʁ	to finish, to end
fournir	fuʁniʁ	to provide
franchir	fʁɑ̃ʃiʁ	to cross, to clear an obstacle
grandir	gʁɑ̃diʁ	to grow up
grossir	gʁosiʁ	to gain weight
guérir	geʁiʁ	to cure
investir	ɛ̃vɛstiʁ	to invest
maigrir	megʁiʁ	to lose weight
nourrir	nuʁiʁ	to feed
obéir	ɔbeiʁ	to obey
punir	pyniʁ	to punish
ralentir	ʁalɑ̃tiʁ	to slow down
réfléchir	ʁefleʃiʁ	to think, to reflect
remplir	ʁɑ̃pliʁ	to fill
réunir	ʁeyniʁ	to reunite
réussir	ʁeysiʁ	to succeed
saisir	seziʁ	to seize, to grasp
vieillir	vjejiʁ	to grow old

Exercises

1. In the following circumstances, would you use *Tu* or *Vous*?

- A child talking to his/her teacher.　　　　□ Tu □ Vous
- A child talking to two friends.　　　　　　□ Tu □ Vous
- A child talking to his/her mother.　　　　 □ Tu □ Vous
- A teenager talking to another teenager.　　□ Tu □ Vous
- A girl talking to her older brothers.　　　 □ Tu □ Vous
- An employee talking to his/her coworker.　□ Tu □ Vous
- A woman talking to her husband.　　　　　□ Tu □ Vous
- A man talking to his children.　　　　　　□ Tu □ Vous
- An old woman talking to her dog.　　　　　□ Tu □ Vous
- A TV host interviewing the Prime Minister.　□ Tu □ Vous

2. Conjugate the following verbs in the indicated form of the present indicative.

ex: Danser, troisième personne du pluriel, féminin (3ʳᵈ person plural, feminine) : Elles dansent.

a)   Habiter, première personne du singulier (1ˢᵗ person singular) :

b)   Finir, deuxième personne du pluriel (2ⁿᵈ person plural) :

c)   Rêver, troisième personne du singulier, <u>féminin</u> (3ʳᵈ person singular, feminine) :

d)   Envahir, première personne du pluriel (1ˢᵗ person plural) :

e)   Montrer, troisième personne du singulier (3ʳᵈ person singular, <u>informal "we"</u>) :

f)   Aider, troisième personne du pluriel, <u>masculin</u> (3ʳᵈ person plural, masculine) :

g)   Réfléchir, deuxième personne du singulier (2ⁿᵈ person singular) :

h)   Trouver, première personne du pluriel (1ˢᵗ person plural) :

i)   Réunir, troisième personne du singulier, <u>masculin</u> (3ʳᵈ person singular, masculine) :

j)   Grossir, troisième personne du pluriel, <u>féminin</u> (3ʳᵈ person plural, feminine) :

6. Present indicative (part 2)

As mentioned in part 1, the third group includes all irregular verbs, whatever the ending of their infinitive. Although third-group verbs are few in number, the ten most frequently used verbs in French all belong to it. It is therefore essential to master their conjugation.

The conjugation of third-group verbs is very varied: this group includes a total of almost **eighty different conjugation patterns**! In this chapter, we present the main irregular verbs, then the main conjugation patterns of the third group.

6.1 Completely irregular verbs

The following verbs follow no pattern of conjugation and can therefore be considered completely irregular. As they follow no conjugation pattern, they must be memorized by heart.

The verb *être* (to be) is obviously the most frequent of French verbs.

PRESENT INDICATIVE / ÊTRE	
Infinitive: *Être (εtʁ)*	English translation
Je **suis** *(sɥi)*	I am
Tu **es** *(ε)*	You are (informal, singular)
Il/Elle/On **est** *(ε)*	He/She is, We are (informal)
Nous **sommes** *(sɔm)*	We are (formal)
Vou̲s **êtes** *(εt)*	You are (plural or formal singular)
Ils/Elles **sont** *(sɔ̃)*	They (m/f) are

The verb *avoir* (to have) is the second most common verb in French.

PRESENT INDICATIVE / AVOIR	
Infinitive: *Avoir (avwaʁ)*	English translation
J'**ai** *(ε)*	I have
Tu **as** *(a)*	You have (informal, singular)
Il/Elle/O̲n **a** *(a)*	He/She has, We have (informal)
Nou̲s **avons** *(avɔ̃)*	We have (formal)
Vou̲s **avez** *(ave)*	You have (plural or formal singular)
Il̲s/Elles **ont** *(ɔ̃)*	They (m/f) have

The verb *aller* (to go) is another example of a completely irregular third-group verb.

PRESENT INDICATIVE / ALLER	
Infinitive: *Aller (ale)*	English translation
Je **vais** *(vε)*	I go
Tu **vas** *(va)*	You go (informal, singular)
Il/Elle/On **va** *(va)*	He/She goes, We go (informal)
Nou̲s **allons** *(alɔ̃)*	We go (formal)
Vou̲s **allez** *(ale)*	You go (plural or formal singular)
Ils/Elles **vont** *(vɔ̃)*	They (m/f) go

Below is a list of the other main third-group verbs with completely irregular conjugation.

⚠ Note that these conjugation patterns usually **also apply to similar verbs**, or to **verbs derived from the base verb**. For example, the conjugation of the verb *faire* (to do) is also that of the verb défaire (to undo). Similar verbs (if any) are listed below each base verb.

PRESENT INDICATIVE / DIRE	
Infinitive: *Dire (diʁ)*	English translation
Je **dis** *(di)*	I say
Tu **dis** *(di)*	You say (informal, singular)
Il/Elle/On **dit** *(di)*	He/She says, We say (informal)
Nous **disons** *(dizɔ̃)*	We say (formal)
Vous **dites** *(dit)*	You say (plural or formal singular)
Ils/Elles **disent** *(diz)*	They (m/f) say

Similar verb: redire.

⚠ The conjugation of the following similar verbs: dédire, maudire, interdire, médire, prédire, contredire, differs in the second person plural: -disez *(dize)*. Ex: *vous médisez, vous prédisez…*

PRESENT INDICATIVE / FAIRE	
Infinitive: *Faire (fɛʁ)*	English translation
Je **fais** *(fɛ)*	I do
Tu **fais** *(fɛ)*	You do (informal, singular)
Il/Elle/On **fait** *(fɛ)*	He/She does, We do (informal)
Nous **faisons** *(føzɔ̃)*	We do (formal)
Vous **faites** *(fɛt)*	You do (plural or formal singular)
Ils/Elles **font** *(fɔ̃)*	They (m/f) do

Similar verbs: défaire, refaire, satisfaire, parfaire, surfaire, contrefaire.

PRESENT INDICATIVE / POUVOIR	
Infinitive: *Pouvoir (puvwaʁ)*	English translation
Je **peux** *(pø)*	I can
Tu **peux** *(pø)*	You can (informal, singular)
Il/Elle/On **peut** *(pø)*	He/She can, We can (informal)
Nous **pouvons** *(puvɔ̃)*	We can (formal)
Vous **pouvez** *(puve)*	You can (plural or formal singular)
Ils/Elles **peuvent** *(pœv)*	They (m/f) can

PRESENT INDICATIVE / SAVOIR	
Infinitive: *Savoir (savwaʁ)*	English translation
Je **sais** *(sɛ)*	I know
Tu **sais** *(sɛ)*	You know (informal, singular)
Il/Elle/On **sait** *(sɛ)*	He/She knows, We know (informal)
Nous **savons** *(savɔ̃)*	We know (formal)
Vous **savez** *(save)*	You know (plural or formal singular)
Ils/Elles **savent** *(sav)*	They (m/f) know

PRESENT INDICATIVE / VALOIR	
Infinitive: *Valoir (valwaʁ)*	English translation
Je **vaux** *(vo)*	I am worth
Tu **vaux** *(vo)*	You are worth (informal, singular)
Il/Elle/On **vaut** *(vo)*	He/She is worth, We are worth (informal)
Nous **valons** *(valɔ̃)*	We are worth (formal)
Vous **valez** *(vale)*	You are worth (plural or formal singular)
Ils/Elles **valent** *(val)*	They (m/f) are worth

Similar verbs: équivaloir, prévaloir.

PRESENT INDICATIVE / VOULOIR	
Infinitive: *Vouloir (vulwaʁ)*	English translation
Je **veux** *(vø)*	I want
Tu **veux** *(vø)*	You want (informal, singular)
Il/Elle/On **veut** *(vø)*	He/She wants, We want (informal)
Nous **voulons** *(vulɔ̃)*	We want (formal)
Vous **voulez** *(vule)*	You want (plural or formal singular)
Ils/Elles **veulent** *(vœl)*	They (m/f) want

Similar verb: revouloir.

PRESENT INDICATIVE / MOURIR	
Infinitive: *Mourir (muʁiʁ)*	English translation
Je **meurs** *(mœʁ)*	I die
Tu **meurs** *(mœʁ)*	You die (informal, singular)
Il/Elle/On **meurt** *(mœʁ)*	He/She dies, We die (informal)
Nous **mourons** *(muʁɔ̃)*	We die (formal)
Vous **mourez** *(muʁe)*	You die (plural or formal singular)
Ils/Elles **meurent** *(mœʁ)*	They (m/f) die

PRESENT INDICATIVE / SERVIR	
Infinitive: *Servir (sɛʁviʁ)*	English translation
Je **sers** *(sɛʁ)*	I serve
Tu **sers** *(sɛʁ)*	You serve (informal, singular)
Il/Elle/On **sert** *(sɛʁ)*	He/She serves, We serve (informal)
Nous **servons** *(sɛʁvɔ̃)*	We serve (formal)
Vous **servez** *(sɛʁve)*	You serve (plural or formal singular)
Ils/Elles **servent** *(sɛʁv)*	They (m/f) serve

Similar verbs: resservir, desservir.

PRESENT INDICATIVE / DORMIR	
Infinitive: *Dormir (dɔʁmiʁ)*	English translation
Je **dors** *(dɔʁ)*	I sleep
Tu **dors** *(dɔʁ)*	You sleep (informal, singular)
Il/Elle/On **dort** *(dɔʁ)*	He/She sleeps, We sleep (informal)
Nous **dormons** *(dɔʁmɔ̃)*	We sleep (formal)
Vous **dormez** *(dɔʁme)*	You sleep (plural or formal singular)
Ils/Elles **dorment** *(dɔʁm)*	They (m/f) sleep

Similar verbs: endormir, rendormir, redormir.

PRESENT INDICATIVE / COURIR	
Infinitive: *Courir (kuʁiʁ)*	English translation
Je **cours** *(kuʁ)*	I run
Tu **cours** *(kuʁ)*	You run (informal, singular)
Il/Elle/On **court** *(kuʁ)*	He/She runs, We run (informal)

Nous **courons** *(kurɔ̃)*	We run (formal)
Vous **courez** *(kuʁe)*	You run (plural or formal singular)
Ils/Elles **courent** *(kuʁ)*	They (m/f) run

Similar verbs: accourir, concourir, encourir, parcourir, recourir, secourir.

PRESENT INDICATIVE / LIRE	
Infinitive: *Lire (liʁ)*	English translation
Je **lis** *(li)*	I read
Tu **lis** *(li)*	You read (informal, singular)
Il/Elle/On **lit** *(li)*	He/She reads, We read (informal)
Nous **lisons** *(lizɔ̃)*	We read (formal)
Vous **lisez** *(lize)*	You read (plural or formal singular)
Ils/Elles **lisent** *(liz)*	They (m/f) read

Similar verbs: relire, élire, réélir.

PRESENT INDICATIVE / RIRE	
Infinitive: *Rire (ʁiʁ)*	English translation
Je **ris** *(ʁi)*	I laugh
Tu **ris** *(ʁi)*	You laugh (informal, singular)
Il/Elle/On **rit** *(ʁi)*	He/She laughs, We laugh (informal)
Nous **rions** *(ʁijɔ̃)*	We laugh (formal)
Vous **riez** *(ʁije)*	You laugh (plural or formal singular)
Ils/Elles **rient** *(ʁi)*	They (m/f) laugh

Similar verb: sourire.

PRESENT INDICATIVE / FUIR	
Infinitive: *Fuir (fɥiʁ)*	English translation
Je **fuis** *(fɥi)*	I flee
Tu **fuis** *(fɥi)*	You flee (informal, singular)
Il/Elle/On **fuit** *(fɥi)*	He/She flees, We flee (informal)
Nous **fuyons** *(fɥijɔ̃)*	We flee (formal)
Vous **fuyez** *(fɥije)*	You flee (plural or formal singular)
Ils/Elles **fuient** *(fɥi)*	They (m/f) flee

Similar verb: s'enfuir.

PRESENT INDICATIVE / PLAIRE	
Infinitive: *Plaire (plɛʁ)*	English translation
Je **plais** *(plɛ)*	I appeal
Tu **plais** *(plɛ)*	You appeal (informal, singular)
Il/Elle/On **plait** *(plɛ)*	He/She appeals, We appeal (informal)
Nous **plaisons** *(plɛzɔ̃)*	We appeal (formal)
Vous **plaisez** *(plɛze)*	You appeal (plural or formal singular)
Ils/Elles **plaisent** *(plɛz)*	They (m/f) appeal

Similar verbs: déplaire, complaire, taire.

PRESENT INDICATIVE / CROIRE	
Infinitive: *Croire (kʁwaʁ)*	English translation
Je **crois** *(kʁwa)*	I believe
Tu **crois** *(kʁwa)*	You believe (informal, singular)
Il/Elle/On **croit** *(kʁwa)*	He/She believes, We believe (informal)
Nous **croyons** *(kʁwajɔ̃)*	We believe (formal)
Vous **croyez** *(kʁwaje)*	You believe (plural or formal singular)
Ils/Elles **croient** *(kʁwa)*	They (m/f) believe

PRESENT INDICATIVE / BOIRE	
Infinitive: *Boire (bwaʁ)*	English translation
Je **bois** *(bwa)*	I drink
Tu **bois** *(bwa)*	You drink (informal, singular)
Il/Elle/On **boit** *(bwa)*	He/She drinks, We drink (informal)
Nous **buvons** *(byvɔ̃)*	We drink (formal)
Vous **buvez** *(byve)*	You drink (plural or formal singular)
Ils/Elles **boivent** *(bwav)*	They (m/f) drink

Similar verb: reboire.

PRESENT INDICATIVE / VOIR	
Infinitive: *Voir (vwaʁ)*	English translation
Je **vois** *(vwa)*	I see
Tu **vois** *(vwa)*	You see (informal, singular)
Il/Elle/On **voit** *(vwa)*	He/She sees, We see (informal)
Nous **voyons** *(vwajɔ̃)*	We see (formal)
Vous **voyez** *(vwaje)*	You see (plural or formal singular)

Ils/Elles **voient** *(vwa)*	They (m/f) see

Similar verbs: revoir, prévoir, entrevoir.

PRESENT INDICATIVE / DEVOIR	
Infinitive: *Devoir (dəvwaʁ)*	English translation
Je **dois** *(dwa)*	I must
Tu **dois** *(dwa)*	You must (informal, singular)
Il/Elle/On **doit** *(dwa)*	He/She must, We must (informal)
Nous **devons** *(dəvɔ̃)*	We must (formal)
Vous **devez** *(dəve)*	You must (plural or formal singular)
Ils/Elles **doivent** *(dwav)*	They (m/f) must

Similar verbs: redevoir.

PRESENT INDICATIVE / VIVRE	
Infinitive: *Vivre (vivʁ)*	English translation
Je **vis** *(vi)*	I live
Tu **vis** *(vi)*	You live (informal, singular)
Il/Elle/On **vit** *(vi)*	He/She lives, We live (informal)
Nous **vivons** *(vivɔ̃)*	We live (formal)
Vous **vivez** *(vive)*	You live (plural or formal singular)
Ils/Elles **vivent** *(viv)*	They (m/f) live

Similar verbs: revivre, survivre.

PRESENT INDICATIVE / SUIVRE	
Infinitive: *Suivre (sɥivʁ)*	English translation
Je **suis** *(sɥi)*	I follow
Tu **suis** *(sɥi)*	You follow (informal, singular)
Il/Elle/On **suit** *(sɥi)*	He/She follows, We follow (informal)
Nous **suivons** *(sɥivɔ̃)*	We follow (formal)
Vous **suivez** *(sɥive)*	You follow (plural or formal singular)
Ils/Elles **suivent** *(sɥiv)*	They (m/f) follow

Similar verbs: s'ensuivre, poursuivre.

PRESENT INDICATIVE / PRENDRE	
Infinitive: *Prendre (pʁɑ̃dʁ)*	English translation
Je **prends** *(pʁɑ̃)*	I take
Tu **prends** *(pʁɑ̃)*	You take (informal, singular)
Il/Elle/On **prend** *(pʁɑ̃)*	He/She takes, We take (informal)
Nous **prenons** *(pʁənɔ̃)*	We take (formal)
Vous **prenez** *(pʁəne)*	You take (plural or formal singular)
Ils/Elles **prennent** *(pʁɛn)*	They (m/f) take

Similar verbs: apprendre, comprendre, détendre, entreprendre, reprendre, surprendre.

PRESENT INDICATIVE / METTRE	
Infinitive: *Mettre (mɛtʁ)*	English translation
Je **mets** *(mɛ)*	I put
Tu **mets** *(mɛ)*	You put (informal, singular)
Il/Elle/On **met** *(mɛ)*	He/She puts, We put (informal)
Nous **mettons** *(mɛtɔ̃)*	We put (formal)
Vous **mettez** *(mɛte)*	You put (plural or formal singular)
Ils/Elles **mettent** *(mɛt)*	They (m/f) put

Similar verbs: admettre, émettre, permettre, promettre, soumettre, transmettre.

6.2 -enir verbs

Third-group verbs ending in *-enir* follow this conjugation pattern:

PRESENT INDICATIVE / -ENIR VERBS	
Infinitive: *Venir (vəniʁ)*	English translation
Je **viens** *(vjɛ̃)*	I come
Tu **viens** *(vjɛ̃)*	You come (informal, singular)
Il/Elle/On **vient** *(vjɛ̃)*	He/She comes, We come (informal)
Nous **venons** *(vənɔ̃)*	We come (formal)
Vous **venez** *(vəne)*	You come (plural or formal singular)
Ils/Elles **viennent** *(vjɛ̃n)*	They (m/f) come

COMMON -ENIR VERBS		
Infinitive	Pronunciation (IPA)	Meaning
tenir	tənik	to hold
maintenir	mɛ̃tnik	to maintain
obtenir	ɔptənik	to obtain
retenir	ʁətənik	to hold back
soutenir	sutnik	to support
devenir	dəvnik	to become
parvenir	paʁvənik	to reach
prévenir	pʁevnik	to prevent
revenir	ʁəvnik	to come back
se souvenir	sə suvnik	to remember

6.3 -tir verbs

Third-group verbs ending in *-tir* follow this conjugation pattern:

PRESENT INDICATIVE / -TIR VERBS	
Infinitive: *Sentir (sɑ̃tik)*	English translation
Je sen**s** *(sɑ̃)*	I smell
Tu sen**s** *(sɑ̃)*	You smell (informal, singular)
Il/Elle/On sen**t** *(sɑ̃)*	He/She smells, We smell (informal)
Nous sen**tons** *(sɑ̃tɔ̃)*	We smell (formal)
Vous sen**tez** *(sɑ̃te)*	You smell (plural or formal singular)
Ils/Elles sen**tent** *(sɑ̃t)*	They (m/f) smell

COMMON -TIR VERBS		
Infinitive	Pronunciation (IPA)	Meaning
consentir	kɔ̃sɑ̃tik	to consent
ressentir	ʁəsɑ̃tik	to feel
mentir	mɑ̃tik	to lie
partir	paʁtik	to leave
sortir	sɔʁtik	to go out

6.4 -ouvrir, offrir, souffrir

Third-group verbs ending in *-ouvrir* , along with verbs *offrir* and *souffrir* actually share the same conjugation pattern as first-group verbs!

PRESENT INDICATIVE / -OUVRIR VERBS + OFFRIR + SOUFFRIR	
Infinitive: *Couvrir (kuvʁiʁ)*	English translation
Je couvre *(kuvʁ)*	I cover
Tu couvres *(kuvʁ)*	You cover (informal, singular)
Il/Elle/On couvre *(kuvʁ)*	He/She covers, We cover (informal)
Nous couvrons *(kuvʁɔ̃)*	We cover (formal)
Vous couvrez *(kuvʁe)*	You cover (plural or formal singular)
Ils/Elles couvrent *(kuvʁ)*	They (m/f) cover

COMMON -OUVRIR VERBS + OFFRIR + SOUFFRIR		
Infinitive	Pronunciation (IPA)	Meaning
ouvrir	uvʁiʁ	to open
rouvrir	ruvʁiʁ	to reopen
découvrir	dekuvʁiʁ	to discover
offrir	ɔfʁiʁ	to offer
souffrir	sufʁiʁ	to suffer

6.5 -cevoir verbs

Third-group verbs ending in *-cevoir* follow this conjugation pattern:

PRESENT INDICATIVE / -CEVOIR VERBS	
Infinitive: *Recevoir (ʁəsəvwaʁ)*	English translation
Je reçois *(ʁəswa)*	I receive
Tu reçois *(ʁəswa)*	You receive (informal, singular)
Il/Elle/On reçoit *(ʁəswa)*	He/She receives, We receive (informal)
Nous recevons *(ʁəsəvɔ̃)*	We receive (formal)
Vous recevez *(ʁəsəve)*	You receive (plural or formal singular)
Ils/Elles reçoivent *(ʁəswav)*	They (m/f) receive

COMMON -CEVOIR VERBS		
Infinitive	Pronunciation (IPA)	Meaning
apercevoir	apɛʁsəvwaʁ	to catch sight of
concevoir	kɔ̃səvwaʁ	to conceive
décevoir	desəvwaʁ	to deceive
percevoir	pɛʁsəvwaʁ	to perceive

6.6 -ondre, -ordre, -erdre, -endre verbs

Third-group verbs ending in *-ondre, -ordre, -erdre* and *-endre* (except verbs ending in *-prendre* ; see above) follow this conjugation pattern:

PRESENT INDICATIVE / -ONDRE, -ORDRE, -ENDRE VERBS	
Infinitive: *Fondre (fɔ̃dʁ)*	English translation
Je fon**ds** *(fɔ̃)*	I melt
Tu fon**ds** *(fɔ̃)*	You melt (informal, singular)
Il/Elle/On fon**d** *(fɔ̃)*	He/She melts, We melt (informal)
Nous fon**dons** *(fɔ̃dɔ̃)*	We melt (formal)
Vous fon**dez** *(fɔ̃de)*	You melt (plural or formal singular)
Ils/Elles fon**dent** *(fɔ̃d)*	They (m/f) melt

COMMON -ONDRE, -ORDRE, -ERDRE, -ENDRE VERBS		
Infinitive	Pronunciation (IPA)	Meaning
répondre	ʁepɔ̃dʁ	to answer
mordre	mɔʁdʁ	to bite
perdre	pɛʁdʁ	to lose
défendre	defɑ̃dʁ	to defend
descendre	desɑ̃dʁ	to go down
entendre	ɑ̃tɑ̃dʁ	to hear
prétendre	pʁetɑ̃dʁ	to pretend
rendre	ʁɑ̃dʁ	to give back
tendre	tɑ̃dʁ	to stretch
vendre	vɑ̃dʁ	to sell

6.7 -eindre verbs

Third-group verbs ending in *-eindre* follow this conjugation pattern:

PRESENT INDICATIVE / -EINDRE VERBS	
Infinitive: *Peindre (pɛ̃dʁ)*	English translation
Je p**eins** *(pɛ̃)*	I paint
Tu p**eins** *(pɛ̃)*	You paint (informal, singular)
Il/Elle/On p**eint** *(pɛ̃)*	He/She paints, We paint (informal)
Nous p**eignons** *(pɛɲɔ̃)*	We paint (formal)
Vous p**eignez** *(pɛɲe)*	You paint (plural or formal singular)
Ils/Elles p**eignent** *(pɛɲ)*	They (m/f) paint

COMMON -EINDRE VERBS		
Infinitive	Pronunciation (IPA)	Meaning
atteindre	atɛ̃dʁ	to attain, to reach
éteindre	etɛ̃dʁ	to turn off
teindre	tɛ̃dʁ	to dye

6.8 -aître verbs

Third-group verbs ending in *-aître* follow this conjugation pattern:

PRESENT INDICATIVE / -AÎTRE VERBS	
Infinitive: *Connaître (kɔnɛtʁ)*	English translation
Je conn**ais** *(kɔnɛ)*	I know
Tu conn**ais** *(kɔnɛ)*	You know (informal, singular)
Il/Elle/On conn**aît** *(kɔnɛ)*	He/She knows, We know (informal)
Nous conn**aissons** *(kɔnesɔ̃)*	We know (formal)
Vous conn**aissez** *(kɔnese)*	You know (plural or formal singular)
Ils/Elles conn**aissent** *(kɔnɛs)*	They (m/f) know

COMMON -AÎTRE VERBS		
Infinitive	Pronunciation (IPA)	Meaning
apparaître	apaʁɛtʁ	to appear
disparaître	dispaʁɛtʁ	to disappear
naître	nɛtʁ	to be born
paraître	paʁɛtʁ	to seem
reconnaître	ʁəkɔnɛtʁ	to recognize

6.9 -crire verbs

Third-group verbs ending in *-crire* follow this conjugation pattern:

PRESENT INDICATIVE / -CRIRE VERBS	
Infinitive: *Écrire (ekʁiʁ)*	English translation
J'**écris** *(ekʁi)*	I write
Tu **écris** *(ekʁi)*	You write (informal, singular)
Il/Elle/On **écrit** *(ekʁi)*	He/She writes, We write (informal)
Nous **écrivons** *(ekʁivɔ̃)*	We write (formal)
Vous **écrivez** *(ekʁive)*	You write (plural or formal singular)
Ils/Elles **écrivent** *(ekʁiv)*	They (m/f) write

COMMON -CRIRE VERBS		
Infinitive	Pronunciation (IPA)	Meaning
décrire	dekʁiʁ	to describe
prescrire	pʁɛskʁiʁ	to prescribe
inscrire	ɛ̃skʁiʁ	to inscribe
souscrire	suskʁiʁ	to subscribe
transcrire	tʁɑ̃skʁiʁ	to transcribe

6.10 -uire verbs

Third-group verbs ending in *-uire* follow this conjugation pattern:

PRESENT INDICATIVE / -UIRE VERBS	
Infinitive: *Cuire (kɥiʁ)*	English translation
Je **cuis** *(kɥi)*	I cook
Tu **cuis** *(kɥiʁ)*	You cook (informal, singular)
Il/Elle/On **cuit** *(kɥiʁ)*	He/She cooks, We cook (informal)
Nous **cuisons** *(kɥizɔ̃)*	We cook (formal)
Vous **cuisez** *(kɥize)*	You cook (plural or formal singular)
Ils/Elles **cuisent** *(kɥiz)*	They (m/f) cook

COMMON -UIRE VERBS		
Infinitive	Pronunciation (IPA)	Meaning
conduire	kɔ̃dɥiʁ	to drive
introduire	ɛ̃tʁɔdɥiʁ	to introduce

produire	pʁɔdɥiʁ	to produce
reproduire	ʁəpʁɔdɥiʁ	to reproduce
séduire	sedɥiʁ	to seduce
traduire	tʁadɥiʁ	to translate
construire	kɔ̃stʁɥiʁ	to build
détruire	detʁɥiʁ	to destruct
nuire	nɥiʁ	to harm

6.11 Falloir, Pleuvoir

The verbs *falloir* and *pleuvoir* (but also the first-group verb *neiger*) are very special verbs. They are used in only one person (the third person masculine singular) and are impersonal (the pronoun *il* does not refer to any person or object). These verbs are known as **defective verbs**.

- The verb *falloir* has no English equivalent. It means "It is necessary to/that…" and is usually followed by the infinitive of another verb: ***Il faut*** *manger* ("It is necessary to eat")
  It can also be followed by the construction *que* + subjunctive (see Chapter 10.6):
  Il faut que tu manges ("It is necessary that you eat")

- The verb *pleuvoir* (to rain) is only used in the following way: ***Il pleut*** (It's raining)

Exercise

Conjugate the following verbs in the indicated form.

ex: Sortir, troisième personne du singulier, féminin (3rd person singular, fem.) : Elle sort.

a) Être, deuxième personne du singulier (2nd person singular) :

b) Avoir, troisième personne du pluriel, masculin (3rd person plural, masc.) :

c) Aller, première personne du singulier (1st person singular) :

d) Pouvoir, troisième personne du singulier, féminin (3rd person singular, fem.) :

e) Servir, deuxième personne du pluriel (2nd person plural) :

f) Lire, deuxième personne du singulier (2nd person singular) :

g) Plaire, première personne du pluriel (1st person plural) :

h) Boire, troisième personne du singulier, masculin (3rd person singular, masc.) :

i) Mettre, deuxième personne du pluriel (2nd person plural) :

j) Soutenir, troisième personne du pluriel, féminin (3rd person plural, fem.) :

k) Partir, deuxième personne du singulier (2nd person singular) :

l) Souffrir, troisième personne du pluriel, masculin (3rd person plural, masc.) :

m) Apercevoir, première personne du singulier (1st person singular) :

n) Rendre, première personne du pluriel (1st person plural) :

o) Éteindre, première personne du singulier (1st person singular) :

p) Naître, deuxième personne du pluriel (2nd person plural) :

q) Traduire, deuxième personne du singulier (2nd person singular) :

7. Forming complex sentences

Congratulations! Now you know:

• How to pronounce French.
• How to agree nouns and adjectives in gender and number.
• How to conjugate verbs in the present indicative tense.

At this stage, you know enough to form simple sentences that you can use in everyday life. Soon enough, you'll feel the need to express more sophisticated ideas. This chapter will complement your existing knowledge by enabling you to form complex sentences in French.

7.1 Negative sentences

Negative sentences in French are formed using the negation particle *ne*, always followed by a complementary negation adverb, usually the word *pas* (not). The sentence structure is as follows:

personal pronoun (or noun)	negation particle	conjugated verb	negation adverb
Je	ne	mange	pas

I eat > *Je mange*
I don't eat > *Je **ne** mange **pas***

There are other negation adverbs that can complement the *ne* particle:

I **never** eat > *Je ne mange **jamais***
I don't eat **anymore** > *Je ne mange **plus***
I don't eat **anything** > *Je ne mange **rien***

I don't see anyone > *Je ne vois **personne***

I don't have any friend > *Je n'ai **aucun** ami*
I don't have any <u>girl</u> friend > *Je n'ai **aucune** amie*

7.2 Interrogative sentences

The structure of basic interrogative sentences is pretty simple:

(article + noun)	conjugated verb	hyphen	personal pronoun	q. mark
Les enfants	dansent	-	ils	?

Are the children dancing? > *Les enfants dansent-ils ?*
Are they dancing? > *Dansent-ils ?*

Is Marie working ? > *Marie travaille-**t**-elle ?**
Are you (plural) sleeping? > *Dormez-vous ?*

* In interrogative sentences, when a conjugated verb is followed by a personal pronoun beginning with a vowel (il, elle, on, ils, elles), a **euphonic t** is added between the verb and the pronoun in order to avoid a hiatus and make the sentence easier to pronounce. This rule doesn't apply to conjugated verbs already ending with a silent t (*Tiennent-elles ?*) or d (*Comprend-il ?*).

7.3 Interrogative adverbs

French interrogative sentences can also be formed using **interrogative adverbs**, such as:

Interrogative adverb	English translation
Comment	How
Quand	When
Où	Where
Quel	What/which
Que	What
Qui	Who
Pourquoi	Why
Combien de	How much / How many
Depuis quand	Since when

When the subject of a question starting with *comment, pourquoi, où, que,* qui, *quand* or *depuis quand* is a **personal pronoun**, the sentence follows the structure below:

interrogative adverb	conjugated verb	hyphen	personal pronoun	question mark
Que	manges	–	tu	?

What are you (sing.) eating? > *Que manges-tu ?*
How is she going? > *Comment va-**t**-elle ?*
Who are you? > *Qui es-tu ?*
Why is he sleeping? > *Pourquoi dort-il ?*
Where do you (plural) live? > *Où vivez-vous ?*
When do you (sing.) want to leave? > *Quand veux-tu partir ?*
Since when have we (informal) been playing tennis? > *Depuis quand joue-**t**-on au tennis ?*

When the subject of a question starting with *quel* or *combien de* is a **personal pronoun**, the structure is as follows:

interrogative adverb	noun	conjugated verb	hyphen	personal pronoun	q. mark
Quel	fruit	manges	-	tu	?

What/Which fruit are you (sing.) eating? > *Quel fruit manges-tu ?*
How much money does she earn? > *Combien d'argent gagne-**t**-elle ?*

When the subject of a question starting with *quel* is a **noun**, the structure is as follows:

interrogative adverb	noun	conjugated verb	q. mark
Quel	enfant	dort	?

What/Which child is sleeping? > *Quel enfant dort ?*
How many brothers does Francis have? > *Combien d'enfants a Francis ?**

* In this example, the noun complement is placed before the verb and the subject after it.

When the subject of a question starting with *que*, *comment* or *où* is a **noun**, the structure is as follows:

interrogative adverb	conjugated verb	(article +) noun	question mark
Que	mangent	les éléphants	?

What do elephants eat? > *Que mangent les éléphants ?*
How is Marie going? > *Comment va Marie ?**
Where does the president live? > *Où vit le président ?*

* The adverb *comment* accepts this structure as well as the following one.

When the subject of a question starting with *comment*, *pourquoi*, *qui*, *quand* or *depuis quand* is a **noun**, the structure is as follows:

interrogative adverb	(article +) noun	conjugated verb	hyphen	personal pronoun	q. mark
Comment	les oiseaux	volent	-	ils	?

How do birds fly? > *Comment les oiseaux volent-ils ?*
Why do stars shine? > *Pourquoi les étoiles brillent-elles ?*
Who does Marie love? > *Qui Marie aime-t-elle ?*
When does Jacques want to leave? > *Quand Jacques veut-il partir ?*
Since when have children been playing tennis? > *Depuis quand les enfants jouent-ils au tennis ?*

→ It is indeed possible to form negative questions in French. To do so, just add the negation particle *ne* **before** the conjugated verb and the negation adverb **after** the conjugated verb (or the personal pronoun, if any). Here are a few examples:

Isn't Marie dancing? > Marie **ne** danse-t-elle **pas** ?
What don't you eat? > *Que **ne** manges-tu **pas** ?*
What/Which fruit does she never eat? > *Quel fruit **ne** mange-t-elle **jamais** ?*
What child doesn't sleep any more? > *Quel enfant **ne** dort **plus** ?*
Why can't moles see anything? > *Pourquoi les taupes **ne** voient-elles **rien** ?*
Why doesn't Paul love anyone? > *Pourquoi Paul **n'**aime-t-il **personne** ?*

7.4 Coordinating conjunctions

Sit back. Relax. The rest of this chapter will be much easier! Let's start with the coordinating conjuctions (*conjonctions de coordination*). Behind this barbaric term lies a well-known type of word: coordinating conjunctions are placed between words, phrases, clauses or sentences of equal grammatical rank.

Here are the most common coordinating conjunctions in French:

Coordinating conjunction	English translation
mais	but
ou*	or
et	and
donc	so
or	but, however
ni	neither/nor
car	because

* Make sure you don't confuse *ou* (or) with *où* (where)

Their use is very similar to that of their English equivalents:
- We are alone but we are happy > *Nous sommes seuls **mais** nous sommes heureux.*
- Does Marie want coffee or tea? > *Marie veut-elle du café **ou** du thé ?*
- I like red and blue > *J'aime le rouge **et** le bleu.*
- He's happy so he sings > *Il est heureux **donc** il chante.*
- I love the piano, but I don't play it > *J'aime le piano, **or** je n'en joue pas.*
- They eat neither meat nor fish > *Ils ne mangent **ni** viande **ni** poisson.*
- You are sad because you are single > *Tu es triste **car** tu es célibataire.*

7.5 Subordinating conjunctions

This type of conjunctions is similar to the previous one, except that subordinating conjunctions (*conjonctions de subordination*) introduce a dependent clause, connecting it to the main clause.

These clauses are linked by **time**, **place**, **causality**, **reason**, **purpose**, **condition** or **contrast**.

Here are the most common subordinating conjunctions in French:

Subordinating conjunction	English translation
que	that
quand	when
lorsque	
avant que, avant de	before
après que	after
pendant que	while
où	where
puisque	since
parce que	because
pour que	in order to
afin de	
bien que	although
si	if

And here's how to use them in a sentence:

- Jeanne is the woman that you love > *Jeanne est la femme **que** tu aimes.*
- I (fem.) am happy when I sing > *Je suis heureuse **quand** je chante.*
- He cries when he's alone > *Il pleure **lorsqu**'il est seul.*
- They (fem.) drink before having dinner > *Elles boivent **avant de** dîner.*
- I work after he's finished > *Je travaille **après qu**'il a terminé.*
- We sleep while they play > *Nous dormons **pendant qu**'ils jouent.*
- They live where they want > *Ils vivent **où** ils veulent.*
- Since you (plural) are here, I'm leaving > ***Puisque** vous êtes là, je pars.*
- She is absent because she is ill > *Elle est absente **parce qu**'elle est malade.*
- I do everything so that you love me > *Je fais tout **pour que** tu m'aimes*.*
- I study in order to have a good job > *J'étudie **afin d**'avoir un bon métier.*
- I laugh although I'm sad > *Je ris **bien que** je sois triste*.*
- Catch me if you can > *Attrape-moi **si** tu peux.*

* These subordinating conjunctions take the subjunctive mood (see Chapter 10.6).

7.6 Prepositions

A preposition is a word that links two parts of a sentence together, specifying the relationship between them. Prepositions can sometimes be used at the beginning of a sentence. The way prepositions work in French is very similar to their English equivalents.

Here are the main French prepositions:

Prepositions	English translation
à*	at, in, to, for
dans	in, inside
par	by, through
pour	for, to
en	in, to, by
vers	towards, near
avec	with
de**	of, from
sans	without, -less
sur	on
sous	under, below

* Followed by *le*, the preposition *à* becomes ***au***. Folllowed by *les*, it becomes ***aux***.
** Followed by *le*, the preposition *de* becomes ***du***. Followed by *les*, it becomes ***des***.

⚠ As in all languages, French prepositions have a wide range of applications.
The examples below are only the most common, and do not form an exhaustive list.

She saw him at the train station > *Elle l'a vu **à** la gare.*
I live in Portugal > *Je vis **au** Portugal.*
We are going to the United States > *Nous allons **aux** États-Unis.*
He says hello to his father > *Il dit bonjour **à** son père.*
House for sale > *Maison **à** louer.*

He's waiting in the car > *Il attend **dans** la voiture.*

I am sending my resignation by mail > *J'envoie ma démission **par** courrier.*
She enters through the door > *Elle entre **par** la porte.*

We eat to live > *Nous mangeons **pour** vivre.*
I work hard for my children > *Je travaille dur **pour** mes enfants.*
I'm leaving for Brazil tomorrow morning > *Je pars **pour** le Brésil demain matin.*

She wants to go to Germany next year > *Elle veut aller **en** Allemagne l'année prochaine.*
We are leaving by car > *Nous partons **en** voiture.*

He's looking towards you > *Il regarde **vers** toi.*
They (fem.) live near the town hall > *Elles vivent **vers** la mairie.*

Are you coming with your sister? > *Viens-tu **avec** ta sœur ?*

I'm not the boss of Michel > *Je ne suis pas le patron **de** Michel.*
Jack comes from the South of the United States > *Jack vient **du** sud **des** États-Unis.*

She reads without her glasses > *Elle lit **sans** ses lunettes.*
I'm homeless > *Je suis **sans** domicile.*

Forks are on the table > *Les fourchettes sont **sur** la table.*
The dog sleeps under a tree > *Le chien dort **sous** un arbre.*

7.7 Adverbs

Unlike adjectives, which modify nouns, adverbs are used to specify or alter the meaning of a **verb**, an **adjective** or an other **adverb**.

Il court vite (he runs fast) > the adverb **vite** modifies the verb *courir*.

Je suis assez lent (I'm quite slow) > the adverb **assez** modifies the adjective *lent*.

Elle ne court pas très vite (she doesn't run very fast) > the adverb **très** modifies the adverb *vite*.

Adverbs can indicate **manner, quantity, intensity, time, place, affirmation, negation** or **doubt** and are most often placed after the word they modify.

Here is a list of the most common adverbs in French:

Type	Adverb	English translation
manner	bien	well
	mal	badly, wrongly
	plutôt	rather
	mieux	better
	comme	like, as
	ensemble	together

quantity/intensity	assez	quite
	beaucoup	a lot
	davantage	more
	environ	about
	moins	less
	peu	little, few
	plus	more
	presque	almost
	tout	all
	si	so
	tellement	
	très	very
	trop	too
time	alors	then
	avant	before
	après	after
	déjà	already
	depuis	since
	encore	again
	enfin	finally
	ensuite	then
	jamais	never
	longtemps	for a long time
	maintenant	now
	parfois	sometimes
	soudain	suddenly
	souvent	often
	toujours	always
place	ailleurs	elsewhere
	devant	in front of
	derrière	behind
	dessous	under
	dessus	on top of
	dehors	outside
	ici	here
	là	there
	loin	far
	partout	everywhere

affirmation	certes	certainly
	vraiment	really
negation	aucun	no
	jamais	never
	rien	nothing
	personne	no one
doubt	apparemment	apparently
	probablement	probably
	sans doute	

→ Adverbs can also be constructed from the **feminine** form of an adjective:

fort (strong)
forte + -**ment** = *fortement* (strongly)

naïf (naïve)
naïve + -**ment** = *naïvement* (naively)

→ Adverbs based on adjectives **ending in a vowel (excluding digraphs/trigraphs)** are constructed from the **masculine** form.

joli (nice) + -ment = *joliment* (nicely)
poli (polite) + -ment = *poliment* (politely)

For epicene adjectives, this question obviously doesn't arise.

→ Adverbs based on adjectives **ending in -ant or -ent** are constructed as follows:

méchant (mean)
mécha- + -mment = *méchamment* (meanly)

bruyant (noisy)
bruya- + -mment = *bruyamment* (noisily)

violent (violent)
viole- + -mment = *violemment* (violently)

fréquent (frequent)
fréque- + -mment = *fréquemment* (frequently)

7.8 Tonic pronouns

Tonic pronouns (*pronoms toniques*) are a class of pronouns used most often:

1. emphatically.

2. after a preposition.

Here is a list of French tonic pronouns:

Tonic pronouns	English translation
moi	me
toi	you
lui, elle	him, her
nous	us
vous	you
eux, elles	them (m/f)

The actual use of tonic pronouns in French is very similar to that of their English equivalents.

1. Emphatic use

Basic sentence: *Je suis français* (I'm French).
Emphatic: *Moi, je suis français* (Me, I am French).

2. Use after a preposition

Ils partent sans toi (They leave without you).
Ce cadeau est pour nous (This gift is for us).
Tu danses avec eux (You dance with them).

Exercise

Translate the following sentences:

a)   I don't want to eat > _____

b)   She never walks > _____

c)   You (sing.) don't sing anymore > _____

d)   Are you (plural) sleeping? > _____

e)   Who wants to drink wine? > _____

f)   Why do children cry? > _____

g) I'm rich but I'm ugly (masc.) > _____

h) We're tired (fem.) so we sleep > _____

i) They're (masc.) interesting because they're smart > _____

j) She studies when she can > _____

k) Children eat in order to grow up > _____

l) You (sing.) don't know where you go > _____

m) He is going to the police station > _____

n) Are you the son of Michel? > _____

o) My mother is jobless > _____

p) I swim rather well > _____

q) My nephew is really funny > _____

r) Do you (plural) sleep outside? > _____

s) She reads slowly > _____

t) <u>You</u> (plural) are weak, but <u>we</u> (fem.) are strong > _____

u) Who is your brother? Him or me? > _____

8. Past tenses

Like most languages, French can use different tenses to describe past events, the choice of tense depending on the nature of the action or state described, and its situation in relation to the present time. In everyday life, French people mainly use two past tenses:

- The *passé composé* ("compound past")
- The *imparfait* (imperfect)

In this chapter, you'll discover these two past tenses and learn when and how to use them.

8.1 Passé composé

The *passé composé* is the tense most frequently used by the French to evoke a past event.

The *passé composé* is used to describe:
- **Specific**, **punctiliar** states or actions **completed** in the past.

As its name suggests, the *passé composé* is a **compound tense**.
In other words, it combines an **auxiliary** verb and a **verb**.

The *passé composé* is constructed as follows:

personal pronoun (or noun)	auxiliary verb (present tense)	past participle of main verb
J'	ai	mangé
Je	suis	parti

J'ai mangé > I ate / I have eaten
Je suis parti > I left / I have left

The two auxiliary verbs in French are ***être*** and ***avoir***. To form the *passé composé*, simply use one of these auxiliaries (almost always *avoir*) conjugated in the **present tense** (see Chapter 6), followed by the **past participle** (*participe passé*) of the main verb.

PASSÉ COMPOSÉ (INDICATIVE)	
Infinitive: *Chanter (ʃɑ̃te)*	English translation
J'ai chanté	I sang
Tu as chanté	You sang
Il/Elle a chanté, On a chanté	He/She sang, We (informal) sang
Nous avons chanté	We sang
Vous avez chanté	You sang
Ils/Elles ont chanté	They sang

How do you know the past participle of a verb?

The past participle of French verbs follows the following pattern:

- First group verbs: verb root + **-é**
  ex : mangé, chanté, dansé, rêvé, pensé…

- *Nous avons mangé* > We ate / We have eaten
  Tu as chanté > You sang / You have sung

- Second group verbs: verb root + **-i**
  ex: choisi, fini, rempli, accueilli…

- *Il a choisi* > He chose / He has chosen
  Vous avez fini > You (plural) finished / You have finished

As always, third-group verbs - because of their irregular nature - are more problematic. To make things easier for you, here's a list of past participles of the most common third-group verbs:

Third-group verb	Past participle
Être	été
Avoir	eu
Aller	allé
Courir*	root + -u *couru, plu, valu, voulu, pu, su, lu, cru, bu, vu, attendu, entendu, répondu, venu, connu, tondu, mordu, perdu, rendu…*
Plaire*	
Valoir*	
Vouloir*	
Pouvoir*	
Savoir*	
Lire*	
Croire*	
Boire*	
Voir*	
Attendre*	
Entendre*	
Répondre	
-enir verbs	
-aître verbs (except naître)	
-ondre, -ordre, -erdre, -endre verbs	

-cevoir verbs	root (ç) + u *reçu, aperçu, déçu, conçu…*
Devoir*	dû
Servir*	root + i *servi, dormi, ri, fui, suivi, senti…*
Dormir	
Rire	
Fuir*	
Suivre*	
-ir verbs	
Dire*	root + it *dit, écrit, cuit, conduit…*
-crire verbs	
-uire verbs	
Faire*	fait
-ouvrir, offrir, souffrir	root + ert *découvert, offert, souffert…*
-eindre verbs	root + eint *peint, atteint, éteint…*
Prendre*	pris
Mettre*	mis
Naître*	né
Vivre*	vécu
Mourir	mort

*As always, similar verbs follow the same pattern as the given verb.

⚠ The past participle of verbs forming the *passé composé* with the *avoir* auxiliary remains invariable, unless it is preceded by a direct object. In this case, the past participle agrees in gender and number **with the direct object**.

ex: *Ils ont écrit une lettre* (They have written a letter).
ex: *La lettre qu'ils ont écrite* (The letter that they have written).

Which verbs form the *passé composé* with the auxiliary *être*?

As mentioned above, almost all French verbs use the verb *avoir* as an auxiliary to form the passé composé: *J'ai mangé, tu as été, il a eu, elle a couru, nous avons dit, vous avez découvert, ils ont peint, elles ont vécu, etc.*

There are, however, a few notable exceptions which actually use the **être** auxiliary.
These are **verbs of "displacement"** (moving from one place to another, literally or figuratively).

Most common verbs of displacement: *Aller, arriver, descendre, monter, mourir, naître, passer, partir, rentrer, sortir, tomber, venir, rester.*

ex: Je suis allé(e), tu es descendu(e), il est monté, elle est morte, on est né(e)s, nous sommes passé(e)s, vous êtes parti(e)(s), ils sont rentrés, elles sont restées.

⚠ Unlike past participles using the *avoir* auxiliary, which remain invariable unless a direct object precedes the verb, past participles using the *être* auxiliary <u>always</u> agree in gender and number **with the subject** (see examples above).

How do you form negative and interrogative sentences in the *passé composé*?

Forming negative sentences in the *passé composé* is very simple:

personal pronoun (or noun)	negation particle	auxiliary verb	negation adverb	past participle
Je	n'	ai	pas	mangé
Mes sœurs	ne	sont	jamais	parties

Je n'ai pas mangé > I didn't eat
Mes sœurs ne sont jamais parties > My sisters have never left
Les villes qu'il n'a pas visitées > The cities that he hasn't visited

Interrogative sentences follow a similar pattern:

(article + noun)	auxiliary verb	hyphen	personal pronoun	past participle	q. mark
Les enfants	ont	-	ils	dansé	?
Michel	est	-	il	sorti	?

Marie a-t-elle travaillé ? > Did Marie work?
Avez-vous dormi ? > Did you (plural) sleep?
Qu'avons-nous mangé ? > What did we eat?

8.2 Imparfait

The ***imparfait*** (imperfect) is the second most common past tense in French.

As its name suggests, the *imparfait* is used to describe:
• **Ongoing** or **habitual** states or actions in the past.

ex: Marie <u>buvait</u> un verre de vin quand je suis arrivé.
Mary was drinking a glass of wine when I arrived.

ex: Quand j'étais petit, j'allais au cinéma avec mon père.
When I was a kid, I used to go to the movies with my dad.

ex: Qui était président des États-Unis en 1990 ?
Who was President of the United States in 1990?

The formation of the *imparfait* is very simple:

1. Take the present stem of the **1ˢᵗ person plural** of a given verb, in the present indicative.
    Ex: nous chantons, nous choisissons, nous prenons.
2. Add the following endings:

IMPERFECT INDICATIVE	
Infinitive: *Chanter (ʃɑ̃te)*	English translation
Je chant**ais**	I was singing / I used to sing
Tu chant**ais**	You were singing / You used to sing
Il/Elle chant**ait**, On chant**ait**	He/She was singing / He/She used to sing We (informal) were singing / We used to sing
Nous chant**ions**	We were singing / We used to sing
Vous chant**iez**	You were singing / You used to sing
Ils/Elles chant**aient**	They were singing / They used to sing

-ais / -ais / -ait / -ions / -iez / -aient
ɛ / ɛ / ɛ / jɔ̃ / je / ɛ

Can you believe it? These conjugation rules and endings are the same for **all French verbs**, regardless of their groups!

2ⁿᵈ group: *Je choisiss**ais**, Tu choisiss**ais**, Il/Elle/On choisiss**ait**, Nous choisiss**ions**, Vous choisiss**iez**, Ils/Elles choisiss**aient**.*

3ʳᵈ group: *Je pren**ais**, Tu pren**ais**, Il/Elle/On pren**ait**, Nous pren**ions**, Vous pren**iez**, Ils/Elles pren**aient**.*

The verb *être* (to be) is the only exception to this rule:

IMPERFECT INDICATIVE / ÊTRE	
Infinitive: *Être (ɛtʁ)*	English translation
J'**étais** *(etɛ)*	I was
Tu **étais** *(etɛ)*	You were
Il/Elle/On **était** *(etɛ)*	He/She was, We (informal) were

Nous **étions** *(etjɔ̃)*	We were
Vous **étiez** *(etje)*	You were
Ils/Elles **étaient** *(etɛ)*	They were

→ The construction of negative or interrogative sentences in the *imparfait* is identical to that of the present indicative.

Je n'aime pas les animaux > Je n'aimais pas les animaux.
Aimes-tu les animaux ? > Aimais-tu les animaux ?
etc.

Exercises

1. Conjugate the following sentences in the *passé composé*.
Ex: Je mange du fromage > J'ai mangé du fromage

a) Elle achète une nouvelle maison > _____

b) Nous oublions ton adresse > _____

c) Achètes-tu du pain ? > _____

d) Ils ne voyagent* jamais en Europe > _____

e) Je réussis mes études > _____

f) Mon père punit ma sœur > _____

g) Vous allez au cinéma > _____

h) Vous ne dites rien > _____

i) La veste que je perds > _____

j) Les filles partent-elles ? > _____

　　*Voyager is <u>not</u> a displacement verb.

2. Translate the following sentences in French, using the *imparfait* tense.
Ex: We were living in Paris > Nous habitions à Paris

a) I was walking fast > _____

b) The birds were flying > _____

c) She used to sing well > _____

d) You (sing.) were filling your glass > _____

e) Our son was growing up > _____

f) We weren't drinking anymore > _____

g) The children were sleeping > _____

h) They (fem.) had a dog > _____

i) You (plural) were unhappy > _____

j) Was she painting? > _____

9. Future tenses

ongratulations! You've now mastered French conjugation in the main present and past tenses. But in life, you sometimes have to look towards the future! As you may have guessed, we're now going to talk about the future in French. French actually uses two types of future tense. Let's find out about each of them, understand their conjugation and when to use them.

9.1 Futur Proche

The *futur proche* ("near future") is used to describe **imminent events** (soon, in a minute, tonight…). As you will see, the structure and meaning of this tense are very similar to the English going to + infinitive.

The *futur proche* is formed using the conjugated verb *aller* (to go), followed by the infinitive:

personal pronoun (or noun)	aller (present indicative)	infinitive of main verb
Je	vais	chanter

Je vais chanter > I'm going to sing
Tu vas bientôt partir > You'll be leaving soon
La fille va répondre > The girl is about to answer

→ The verb *aller* applies to **all verbs without exception**, including verbs of displacement: *Ils vont partir, L'enfant va naître, Nous allons descendre*, etc.

→ The formation of negative or interrogative sentences in the *futur proche* follows the same pattern as for the *passé composé* (see Chapter 8), with the verb aller in the position of auxiliary.

Je n'ai pas mangé > *Je ne vais pas manger*
Les enfants ont-ils dansé ? > *Les enfants vont-ils danser ?*

9.2 Futur Simple

The *futur simple* ("future simple") is used to describe events that will happen in a – more or less – **distant future**: tomorrow, next week, next month, in ten years, etc.

The conjugation of the *futur simple* proceeds as follows:

1. Take the **infinitive** of any given verb.
   ex: Chanter, Choisir, Prendre.

2. Add the following endings:

FUTUR SIMPLE (INDICATIVE)	
Infinitive: *Chanter (ʃɑ̃te)*	English translation
Je chanter**ai**	I will sing
Tu chanter**as**	You will sing
Il/Elle chanter**a**, On chanter**a**	He/She will sing We (informal) will sing
Nous chanter**ons**	We will sing
Vous chanter**ez**	You will sing
Ils/Elles chanter**ont**	They will sing

-ai / **-as** / **-a** / **-ons** / **-ez** / **-ont**
ɛ / a / a / ɔ̃ / e / ɔ̃

Here are a few more details on pronunciation and conjugation in the *futur simple* tense:

→ The pronunciation of the last syllable of the infinitive of first-group verbs (ex: *chanter*) changes from e to ə when the infinitive is used to form the future simple. In addition, the silent R becomes audible.

Chanter ʃɑ̃*te* > *je chanterai (ʃɑ̃təʁɛ), tu chanteras (ʃɑ̃təʁa), etc.*
Danser dɑ̃se > *je danserai (dɑ̃səʁɛ), tu danseras (dɑ̃səʁa), etc.*

→ When an **e** (pronounced ə) is present in the last syllable of the root of an infinitive (ex: *peser, acheter*), it becomes **è** in the future simple tense, as in the present indicative (see Chapter 5).

Peser pəze > *je pèserai (pɛzəʁɛ), tu pèseras (pɛzəʁa), etc.*
Acheter aʃəte > *j'achèterai (aʃɛtəʁɛ), tu achèteras (aʃɛtəʁa), etc.*

→ The final consonant of many **-eler/-eter verbs** is doubled. Pronunciation is thus modified.

Appeler apəle > *j'appellerai (apɛləʁɛ), tu appelleras (apɛləʁa), etc.*
Jeter ʒəte > *je jetterai (ʒɛtəʁɛ), tu jetteras (ʒɛtəʁa), etc.*

Notable exceptions: *acheter, geler, modeler…*

→ The **y** in **-yer verbs** becomes an **i**.

Payer > *je paierai, tu paieras, etc.*
Nettoyer > *je nettoierai, tu nettoieras, etc.*

Notable exceptions: *envoyer, renvoyer (see below).*

→ For third-group **verbs ending in -e**, the final -e disappears from the infinitive root.
Je prendrai, tu prendras, il/elle/on prendra, nous prendrons, vous prendrez, ils prendront.

→ The i in the verbs **courir** and **mourir** disappears in the *futur simple* tense.
Make sure you pronounce the two successive r's.

Courir kuʁiʁ > *je courrai (kuʁʁɛ), tu courras (kuʁʁa), etc.*
Mourir muʁiʁ > *je mourrai (muʁʁɛ), tu mourras (muʁʁa), etc.*

Irregular verbs

Pretty simple, right? But what would French be without its infamous irregular verbs? Rest assured, all you need to know is the irregular root of the *futur simple* of these verbs. The endings are then perfectly regular.

Here are the main irregular verbs in the *futur simple* tense:

ÊTRE: *Je serai, tu seras, il/elle/on sera, nous serons, vous serez, ils/elles seront.*

AVOIR: *J'aurai, tu auras, il/elle/on aura, etc.*

ALLER: *J'irai, tu iras, etc.*

ENVOYER: *J'enverrai, tu enverras, etc.*

FAIRE: *Je ferai, tu ferais, etc.*

POUVOIR: *Je pourrai, tu pourras, etc.*

SAVOIR: *Je saurai, tu sauras, etc.*

VALOIR: *Je vaudrai, tu vaudras, etc.*

VOULOIR: *Je voudrai, tu voudras, etc.*

VOIR: *Je verrai, tu verras, etc.*

DEVOIR: *Je devrai, tu devras, etc.*

VENIR: *Je viendrai, tu viendras, etc.*

TENIR: *Je tiendrai, tu tiendras, etc.*

RECEVOIR: *Je <u>rece</u>vrai, tu recevras, etc.*

FALLOIR: *Il faudra.*

PLEUVOIR: *Il pleuvra.*

⚠ As always, these conjugation patterns also apply to similar verbs, or to verbs derived from the base verb. Thus, the irregular *futur simple* root of the verb *venir* (to come) is also that of the verb *devenir* (to become) or *prévenir* (to prevent): *Je <u>vien</u>drai* ; je <u>devien</u>drai ; je <u>prévien</u>drai, etc.

Exercise

Translate the following sentences into French, using the appropriate future tense (*futur proche* or *futur simple*):

a) *They (fem.) will never grow up* > _____

b) *I'll eat a lot tonight (ce soir)* > _____

c) *She will arrive soon* > _____

d) *In ten years, we'll be rich* > _____

e) *I'll go to church tomorrow* > _____

f) *The movie (le film) is about to start* > _____

g) *We'll call you in a week* > _____

h) *He will pay next month (le mois prochain)* > _____

i) *One day, Earth (la terre) will disappear* > _____

j) *You'll receive my letter (lettre) in five days* > _____

k) *It's going to rain* > _____

l) *It will be necessary to run* > _____

10. Moods

You now have a solid grounding in everyday French. So that you can continue your linguistic journey on your own, we'd like to close this manual by introducing you to the other moods of French, which will enable you to form more sophisticated sentences and express a wider range of intentions and feelings.

10.1 Introduction to moods

In grammar, moods are verb forms that express the speaker's attitude towards the action or state defined by the verb. French has seven moods. You already know three of them:

- *L'infinitif* (infinitive) – This is the **basic form** of the verb.
  ex: manger, finir, prendre, vouloir, etc.

- *L'indicatif* (indicative) – The mood of **factual statements** and **positive beliefs**.
  The various tenses that you have learned in the previous chapters are all indicative.

- *Le participe* (participle) – A verb form that can be used as a **verb**, as a **noun**, as an **adjective**, as well as to form **compound tenses**, the **passive voice** or the **gerund**.

  In this chapter, you'll discover the second type of participle, and the other four moods of French:

- *Le gérondif* (gerund) – A verb form used to indicate the **circumstances** of an action or state.

- *L'impératif* (imperative) – The mood used to express **orders**, **requests** or **prohibitions**.

- *Le conditionnel* (conditional) – The mood of **hypothetical situations** dependent on certain conditions, or **polite requests**.

- *Le subjonctif* (subjunctive) – The mood of **doubts**, **emotions**, **wishes** or **possibilities**.

10.2 Le participe

There are two types of participles in French:

- The ***participe présent*** (present participle), describing ongoing actions or states.
- The ***participe passé*** (past participle), describing past actions or states.

Being already familiar with the past participle (see chapter 8), we now turn to the present participle. The *participe présent* is formed as follows:

1. Take the present indicative stem of the **1ˢᵗ person plural** of a given verb.

ex: nous <u>mangeons</u>, nous <u>finissons</u>, nous <u>prenons</u>, etc.

2. Add the suffix **-ant**.
   *ex: mange**ant**, finiss**ant**, pren**ant**, etc.*

Is that all? Yes, it is! And this pattern works for all verbs, regardless of their group, with the exception of just three verbs:

ÊTRE > étant

AVOIR > ayant

SAVOIR > sachant

Verbal use of the participe présent

When used as a verb, the French present participle basically perform the same function as its English equivalent. It is most often used to describe an **ongoing action or state** taking place **at the same time** as the main verb of the sentence (usually conjugated in an indicative tense).

J'ai vu un homme <u>courant</u> dans le jardin
I saw a man <u>running</u> in the garden

It can also indicate **the cause** behind the action or state described by the main verb.

<u>Voulant</u> changer de vie, Jacques a quitté la France
<u>Wanting</u> to change his life, Jacques left France

Or **the outcome** of the action or state described by the main verb.

Jacques a quitté la France, <u>finissant</u> sa vie au Canada
Jacques left France, <u>ending</u> his life in Canada

Non-verbal uses of the participle

As mentioned above, participles can also be used as **nouns**.

Examples – *participe présent*
Étudier (to study) > un étu<u>diant</u> (a student)
Gagner (to win) > un gagn<u>ant</u> (a winner)

Examples – *participe passé*
Inviter (to invite) > un invit<u>é</u> (a guest)

Exposer (to present) > un exposé (a presentation)

→ When used as nouns to designate human beings, participles **agree in gender and number,** just like any other noun in French:

Un étudiant, des étudiants, une étudiante, des étudiantes.
Un gagnant, des gagnants, une gagnante, des gagnantes.
Un invité, des invités, une invitée, des invitées.

As your French vocabulary grows, you'll discover that many French nouns are actually substantivized past or present participles!

In a similar way, participles can be used as **adjectives.**

Examples – *participe présent*
Ignorer (to ignore) > ignorant (ignorant)
Sourire (to smile) > souriant (smiley)

Examples – *participe passé*
Priver (to deprive) > privé (private)
Perdre (to lose) > perdu (lost)

→ When used as adjectives, participles **agree in gender and number** with the noun they modify, just like any other adjective in French:

Des enfants ignorants
Une femme souriante
Des toilettes privées
Une chatte perdue, etc.

Compound tenses

French compound tenses are all formed in the following way:

personal pronoun (or noun)	auxiliary verb (être or avoir)	past participle of main verb

Only the <u>mood or tense of the auxiliary verb</u> distinguishes the various **compound tenses**:

P.pronoun/noun + <u>present indicative</u> + past participle of the main verb = ***passé composé***

J'ai mangé > I have eaten

P.pronoun/noun + <u>imperfect indicative</u> + past participle of the main verb = ***plus-que-parfait***

J'avais mangé > I had eaten

P.pronoun/noun + <u>future indicative</u> + past participle of the main verb = ***futur antérieur***

J'aurai mangé > I will have eaten

P.pronoun/noun + <u>present conditional</u> + past participle of the main verb = ***conditionnel passé***

J'aurais mangé > I would have eaten

P.pronoun/noun + <u>present subjunctive</u> + past participle of the main verb = ***subjonctif passé***

(Que) J'aie mangé > (That) I ate

⚠ There are a few other compound tenses in French, reserved for a more literary use.

The passive voice

In addition to compound tenses, the past participle is also used to construct the **passive voice**. The passive voice is the verbal form in which the subject of a sentence **receives the action** of the main verb, rather than performing it.

Active voice: *Jeanne peint la maison (Jeanne paints the house).*

Passive voice: *La maison est peinte par Jeanne (The house is painted by Jeanne).*

The formation of the passive voice in French is very simple:

Tense	personal pronoun (or noun)	auxiliary verb (for compound tenses)	auxiliary verb: être	past participle of main verb
Présent	Je		suis	perdu
Imparfait	Marie		était	perdue
Passé composé	Nous (fem)	avons	été	perdues
Futur simple	Les chiens		seront	perdus

→ The above tenses are all indicative. The other indicative tenses and the other moods (conditional, subjunctive...) all use the *être* auxiliary to form their passive voice.

⚠ Since it is preceded by the *être* auxiliary, the past participle of the main verb <u>always</u> **agrees in gender and number** with the subject of the sentence in the passive voice.

10.3 Le gérondif

The *gérondif* (gerund) is a verb form used **to indicate the circumstances** of the action or state expressed by the main verb of a sentence.

The ***gérondif présent*** is formed in the following way:

The preposition **en + present participle**.
Ex: en mangeant, en finissant, en prenant, etc.

The ***gérondif passé*** is formed in the following way:

en + present participle of avoir auxiliary + past participle.
Ex: en ayant mangé, en ayant fini, en ayant pris, etc.

→ In the *gérondif*, both present and past participles <u>never</u> agree in gender and number, with the sole exception of the case described below.

⚠ As usual, verbs of displacement take the *être* auxiliary instead of *avoir*. In this case, the present participle remains invariable, but the past participle agrees in gender and number. *Ex: en étant devenus, en étant partie, en étant sorties, etc.*

Functions of the gérondif

The functions of the *gérondif* are similar to those of the participle, except that the *gérondif* always applies to **the subject** of the sentence.

PARTICIPE PRÉSENT
J'ai vu un homme <u>courant</u> dans le jardin
I saw a man <u>running</u> in the garden (the man is the one running)

GÉRONDIF PRÉSENT
J'ai vu un homme <u>en courant</u> dans le jardin
I saw a man <u>while running</u> in the garden (I am the one running)

In addition to **simultaneity** (see above), the *gérondif* can also indicate the **condition** for the action or state described by the main verb to take place:

<u>En nous levant tôt</u>, nous serons à l'heure
<u>By getting up early</u>, we'll be on time

Or the **cause** or **manner**:

Elle est tombée <u>en réparant</u> le toit
She fell <u>while fixing</u> the roof

Beethoven est mort <u>en ayant composé neuf symphonies</u>
Beethoven died <u>having composed</u> nine symphonies

10.4 L'impératif

The function of the French *impératif* (imperative) is exactly the same as its English equivalent. This mood is used to express **requests** or **orders**, in a more or less authoritative way, depending on the context.

⚠ There are two tenses in the imperative mood: the *impératif présent* (present imperative) and the *impératif passé* (past imperative), but the latter is way too rare and literary to mention here.

To form the **2nd person singular** of the present imperative, take the 2nd person singular of the present indicative, then remove the pronoun and the final S:

Tu manges > Mange ! (Eat!)

The **1st person plural** of the present imperative is identical to the present indicative (without the pronoun):

Nous partons > Partons ! (Let's leave!)

Same thing for the **2nd person plural**:

Vous venez > Venez ! (Come!)

Only three verbs are exceptions to this rule:

ÊTRE
2nd person singular: *Sois*
1st person plural: *Soyons*
2nd person plural: *Soyez*

AVOIR
2nd person singular: *Aie*
1st person plural: *Ayons*
2nd person plural: *Ayez*

SAVOIR
2nd person singular: *Sache*

1st person plural: *Sachons*
2nd person plural: *Sachez*

→ The *impératif présent* is often used in the negative form to express a **prohibition**:

Ne touche pas ! (Don't touch!)
Ne dites rien ! (Say nothing!)

⚠ When travelling in a French-speaking country, you may come across public signs expressing a prohibition using the infinitive instead of the imperative – *Ex: Ne pas fumer (No smoking).* Fortunately, this strange imperative use of the infinitive only occurs in this very specific case!

10.5 Le conditionnel

The *conditionnel* (conditional) has several functions in French.

The main one is to refer to **hypothetical events or situations**.

In this case, the verb conjugated in a conditional tense (most often the *conditionnel présent*) generally takes its place in a conditional sentence beginning with the subordinating conjunction **si**, potentially followed by the adverb **alors** (See chapter 7).

Here is the structure of a typical conditional sentence in French:

Si	*Imparfait* clause	(alors), explicit or implied	*Conditionnel présent* clause
Si	j'étais riche	(alors)	je serais heureux

Si j'étais riche, (alors) je serais heureux.
If I were rich, (then) I would be happy.

Si tu voulais grossir, (alors) tu mangerais.
If you wanted to put on weight, (then) you'd eat.

S'ils buvaient moins, (alors) ils pourraient conduire.
If they drank less, (then) they could drive.

As you may have noticed, the conjugation of the *conditionnel présent* is very similar to that of the *imparfait* (see chapter 8). This is no coincidence. In fact, the formation of the *conditionnel présent* is quite simple:

1. Take the *futur simple* stem of a given verb (see Chapter 9).
   ex: je mangerai, tu finiras, il prendra, etc.

2. Add the *imparfait* endings.
   ex: mangeais, finissais, il prenait, etc.

So, this is how it looks like:

Je + manger + ais = *Je mangerais* (I would eat)
Tu + finir + ais = *Tu finirais* (You would finish)
Il + prendr + ait = *Il prendrait* (He would take)

That's all! And, believe it or not: there are **no exceptions** to this rule. Just make sure you're familiar with the *futur simple* stems, which are sometimes irregular (see Chapter 9).

Here's a complete pattern for the present conditional, just so we're clear:

PRESENT CONDITIONAL	
Infinitive: *Chanter (ʃɑ̃te)*	English translation
Je chanter**ais**	I would sing
Tu chanter**ais**	You would sing
Il/Elle/On chanter**ait**	He/She/We would sing
Nous chanter**ions**	We would sing
Vous chanter**iez**	You would sing
Ils/Elles chanter**aient**	They would sing

⚠ The conditional mood is made up of two tenses: the *conditionnel présent* (above) and the *conditionnel passé*, rarer but still used quite frequently. Once you're comfortable with the content of this beginners' manual, the *conditionnel passé* is one of the tenses that you'll have to study to continue your language learning journey.

Other uses of the conditional

Like its English equivalent (would + verb), the French conditional can be used for purposes other than evoking a hypothetical situation:

• As a **politeness marker**, with verbs of will (*vouloir, souhaiter, aimer, désirer...*)
  Je veux une tasse de café (I want a cup of coffee) > rude
  J'aimerais une tasse de café, s'il vous plaît (I'd like a cup of coffee, please) > polite

• To **give an advice**, with the verb *devoir* or the idiomatic *faire mieux de*
  Tu devrais boire moins d'alcool (You should drink less alcohol)
  Elle ferait mieux de faire du sport (She'd better do some sport)

- To **express a wish**, with the verb *aimer* (or *adorer*)
  J'aimerais te revoir (I'd like to see you again)
  Nous adorerions visiter Paris (We'd love to visit Paris)

- To talk about an **imaginary fact**, more or less realistic
  Je serais plus heureux à la campagne (I'd be happier in the country)

10.6 Le subjonctif

The *subjonctif* (subjunctive) is perhaps the most difficult mood for a learner of French to understand. It has no real equivalent in English, and its endings can be puzzling. The *subjonctif* is used to express **wishes, emotions, doubts** and **possibilities**.

The subjunctive is almost always introduced by the subordinating conjunction ***que***.

Il aimerait que tu l'aimes
He'd like (that) you love him

Je doute qu'ils acceptent
I doubt (that) they'll accept

Nous sommes tristes que Jean soit parti
We are sad that Jean has gone

⚠ Although the subjunctive mood comprises four tenses in all (two of which are only used in writing), in this beginners' manual we'll confine ourselves to introducing you to the *subjonctif présent*. As with the conditional, we strongly recommend that you learn the *subjonctif passé* later on, in order to perfect and deepen your knowledge of French.

How do you conjugate a verb in the *subjonctif présent*?

The basic conjugation of the *subjonctif présent* is relatively simple:

- Take the present indicative stem of the **3rd person plural** of a given verb.
  ex: ils mangent, ils finissent, ils vendent, etc.

- Add the appropriate present subjunctive ending.
  -e, -es, -e, -ions, -iez, -ent.

Here's a concrete example:

PRESENT SUBJUNCTIVE	
Infinitive: *Chanter (ʃɑ̃te)*	English translation
(Que) je chant**e**	(That) I sing
(Que) Tu chant**es**	(That) You sing
(Qu') Il/Elle/On chant**e**	(That) He/She/We sing
(Que) Nous chant**ions**	(That) We sing
(Que) Vous chant**iez**	(That) You sing
(Qu') Ils/Elles chant**ent**	(That) They sing

Although this rule applies to **the vast majority of third-group verbs**, there are still some verbs with irregular subjunctives, whose stem is sometimes far removed from the indicative. We can distinguish two types of irregular subjunctive:

1. **Dual-stem irregular subjunctive forms**

The following verbs obey the rule described above, with the exception of the 1st and 2nd person plurals, which are based on the present indicative stem of their respective person.

VENIR: *(Que) je vienne, tu viennes, il/elle/on vienne, nous <u>venions</u>, vous <u>veniez</u>, ils viennent.*

PRENDRE: *(Que) je prenne, tu prennes, il/elle/on prenne, nous <u>prenions</u>, vous <u>preniez</u>, ils prennent.*

BOIRE: *(Que) je boive, tu boives, il/elle/on boive, nous <u>buvions</u>, vous <u>buviez</u>, ils boivent.*

The following verbs have two stems as well, but the main stem (and sometimes both) differs significantly from the indicative.

ÊTRE: *(Que) je sois, tu sois, il/elle/on soit, nous <u>soyons</u>, vous <u>soyez</u>, ils soient.*

AVOIR: *(Que) j'aie, tu aies, il/elle/on ait, nous <u>ayons</u>, vous <u>ayez</u>, ils aient.*

ALLER: *(Que) j'aille, tu ailles, il/elle/on aille, nous <u>allions</u>, vous <u>alliez</u>, ils aillent.*

VOULOIR: *(Que) je veuille, tu veuilles, il/elle/on veuille, nous <u>voulions</u>, vous <u>vouliez</u>, ils viennent.*

VALOIR: *(Que) je vaille, tu vailles, il/elle/on vaille, nous <u>valions</u>, vous <u>valiez</u>, ils vaillent.*

2.   Single-stem irregular subjunctive forms

The following verbs are based on a single stem, which is completely different from the indicative. As with the other irregular subjunctives, however, their endings are perfectly regular.

FAIRE: *(Que) je fasse, tu fasses, il/elle/on fasse, nous fassions, vous fassiez, ils fassent.*

POUVOIR: *(Que) je puisse, tu puisses, il/elle/on puisse, nous puissions, vous puissiez, ils puissent.*

SAVOIR: *(Que) je sache, tu saches, il/elle/on sache, nous sachions, vous sachiez, ils sachent.*

PLEUVOIR: *(Qu') il pleuve.*

FALLOIR: *(Qu') il faille.*

Exercises

1. Conjugate the following verbs in the given mood and tense.

Ex: Manger, participe présent > mangeant

a)   Finir, gérondif présent > _____
b)   Être, impératif, 2nd person plural > _____
c)   Aller, gérondif passé > _____
d)   Savoir, participe présent > _____
e)   Avoir, impératif, 2nd person singular > ____

2. Translate the following sentences using the *conditionnel présent* when needed.

a)   I'd love to travel > _____
b)   If I were poor, I would be sad > _____
c)   She'd better eat less meat > _____
d)   We'd like a cup of tea, please > _____
e)   You (plural) should go out > _____

3. Conjugate the indicated verb in the *subjonctif présent* to fill in the blank.
Ex: (savoir) Je veux que tu saches que je t'aime.

a)   (être) Elle est heureuse que vous _____ là.
b)   (pouvoir) Je ne suis pas sûr qu'ils _____ venir.
c)   (venir) Nous aimerions que tu _____ avec nous.
d)   (parler) Je ne savais pas que vous _____ japonais !
e)   (vendre) Sa femme veut qu'il _____ sa voiture.

French Phrasebook For

Beginners

Learn Common Phrases In Context With
Explanations For Everyday Use and Travel

Worldwide Nomad

Chapter 1
Greeting in French

The Basics

Hello and welcome to this chapter exploring the art of French greetings. Greetings play a crucial role in our daily lives, enabling us to form a bond and express our politeness to others.

Introducing yourself in France or other French-speaking countries involves expressing politeness, warmth, and a genuine desire to connect with others. Unlike some North American or European countries, French people are generally open to getting to know others and will treat you as a friend from the start.

Here's a short guide to help you introduce yourself in a French or francophone context, as well as a useful phrase to start a pleasant conversation:

- When you meet someone for the first time:
- Greet them with a warm smile and say "Bonjour" (Hello) or "Bonsoir" (Good evening), depending on the time of day.

- To introduce yourself:
- Say "Je m'appelle [Your Name]" (My name is [Your Name]).

- To ask for the other person's name:
- You can say «Et vous, comment vous appelez-vous?» (And you, what's your name?) or simply "Comment vous appelez-vous?" (What's your name?).

- To express interest in getting to know the other person:
- You can say "Enchanté(e)" (Nice to meet you) or "Ravi(e) de faire votre connaissance" (Pleased to meet you).

- To start a conversation:
- A good conversation starter is «Qu'est-ce que vous faites dans la vie?» (What do you do for a living?). This shows interest in the other person and invites them to share more about themselves.

Remember to maintain eye contact, listen actively, and engage in a friendly conversation. Enjoy getting to know new people in a French or francophone setting!

Start with a Greeting

When you meet someone for the first time, it's important to make a good impression right from the start. A warm greeting can break the ice and create a feeling of welcome. In French, the most common greeting is "Bonjour", which simply translates as "hello" in English. However, there are other greetings you can use depending on the time of day.

In the morning, you can say "Bonjour" to say good morning, but if you want to be more specific, you can add "Bon matin" to say "bonne journée". In the afternoon, you can say "Bon après-midi", and in the evening, you can use "Bonsoir" to say good night.

In addition to the usual greetings, it's important to know the polite expressions in French. For example, when you enter a store, it's common to say "Bonjour" or "Bonsoir" to employees to show your respect. Similarly, when you leave a place, it's polite to say "Au revoir" to say goodbye.

In more formal situations, you can use expressions like "Enchanté" to say "delighted to meet you" or "Comment ça va?" to ask how things are going. These expressions show that you're polite and that you care about the other person.

It's also important to know the differences between greeting expressions for men and women in French. For example, when you greet a man, you can say "Bonjour, Monsieur" and when you greet a woman, you can say "Bonjour, Madame". This also shows your respect for the other person.

In the workplace, greetings play an essential role. When you enter a meeting or an interview, you should greet your colleagues or employers appropriately. Expressions such as "Hello, how are you?" or "Nice to meet you" show your professionalism and commitment.

It's also important to consider cultural and regional traditions when it comes to greetings. For example, in some parts of France, it's customary to give a kiss as a greeting, while in other regions or in a professional context, a handshake is more appropriate.

Use Formal Titles

If you find yourself in a formal setting, it is essential to address the people in question, using their surnames, as follows :

- "Monsieur" for Mr.
- "Madame" for Mrs.

In this formal setting, you should follow this protocol until the person concerned gives you permission to call them by their first name.

By way of example, here are some formal greetings you can use:

Good morning, Mr. Jack
Bonjour, Monsieur Jack

Good evening, Mrs. Clara
Bonsoir, Madame Clara

Very pleased to greet you, Mr. and Mrs. Dubois!
Très heureux de vous saluer, M. et Mme Dubois !

Express Politeness

Politeness is highly valued in French culture. Even though people may greet with kisses on the cheeks or have more physical interactions, it is important to use polite expressions and manners. Respect personal space and let others speak first. Avoid interrupting someone when they are speaking and always use polite expressions such as "s'il vous plait" (please) and "merci" (thank you) frequently.

When eating at a table, it is important to ask for permission:

1. Have more food or drinks:
   Puis-je avoir plus de poulet/limonade/salade/riz s'il vous plaît ?
   Can I have more chicken/lemonade/salad/rice please?

2. Leave the table:
   Excusez-moi, je dois aller aux toilettes/répondre à cet appel.
   Excuse me, I need to go to the restroom/answer this call.

3. Interrupt the person speaking:
   Puis-je dire quelque chose ? or J'aimerais dire quelque chose.
   Can I say something? or I would like to say something.

(Do not) Be Mindful of Time

French culture also has a more relaxed attitude towards time. Don't worry too much about punctuality and expect conversations to take their natural course. If you need to leave, it is recommended to inform your hosts or the people you are with in advance so that they are aware of your time constraints.

For example:

Je dois partir dans 30 minutes pour attraper mon bus.
I need to leave in 30 minutes to catch my bus.
Je dois rentrer à mon hôtel/chez moi dans 30 minutes pour me reposer.
I have to go back to my hotel/home in 30 minutes to rest.

Know that giving a 30-minute notice is considered the best way to announce that you cannot stay longer. Also, be aware that events in France often start later than the established time. Being punctual is not as important in French culture, and most people are aware of this.

Hands and Arms

Using gestures and hand movements is common in French communication. Do not be afraid to use gestures when speaking French, as they can enrich conversations and make them more vivid. However, be mindful of respecting others' personal space while using gestures.

Engage in Small Talk

Small talk is a great way to break the ice in French culture. If you ask someone how they are, expect a more detailed response than just "good." Asking about someone's day, family, or interests is a common way to start a conversation and show genuine interest in the other person.

If you want to start a conversation or make a new friend, ask about their day, family, or interests. Common topics include family, hobbies, and cultural events. French people are passionate about these topics and enjoy discussing them. Here are some useful phrases:

Comment allez-vous? (formal) / Comment tu vas? (informal)
How are you?

Comment s'est passé votre week-end? (formal) / Comment s'est passé ton week-end? (informal)
How was your weekend?

Comment va votre famille? (formal) / Comment va ta famille? (informal)
How is your family doing?

Qu'aimez-vous faire pendant votre temps libre? (formal) / Qu'aimes-tu faire pendant ton temps libre? (informal)
What do you like doing in your free time?

Use Formal Language

In French, there is a distinction between formal and informal language. Use the formal pronoun "vous" when addressing others in formal settings or when speaking to older individuals or those in positions of authority. Once you have established a level of familiarity, you may switch to using the informal pronoun "tu".

For example:
Tu es mon meilleur ami(e). / Vous êtes mon meilleur ami(e).
You are my best friend.

Until you are familiar with the level of formality in a particular setting, it is advisable to use formal language and address others with vous. This is especially true when speaking to older individuals or those in positions of authority. Once you have gained someone's trust, they may invite you to use tu, which signifies a closer relationship.

Learn Basic Phrases in French

While many French people speak English, making an effort to communicate in French will be appreciated. Learning basic phrases in French can help you navigate daily interactions and show respect for the language and culture.

Show Genuine Interest

Demonstrating genuine interest and curiosity in French culture will be appreciated by locals. Asking open-ended questions and actively listening to responses can help you engage in meaningful conversations and connect with others on a deeper level.

Participate in Cultural Customs

When in France, try to participate in specific cultural customs or traditions. Locals expect and appreciate your participation in activities, such as sharing a traditional meal or attending local events or dances. Involvement fosters a sense of connection and allows you to fully experience the local culture. While it's not mandatory to participate, it is highly encouraged as it shows your willingness to embrace and learn from the local customs and traditions.

Remember, every region in France has its own unique customs and nuances. Be adaptable, observant, and approach introductions with respect, an open mind, and a willingness to embrace the local culture.

Chapter 2
Transportation

Now, it's time to learn essential words and phrases for English speakers who are learning French. In this chapter, we will explore the dynamic world of introductions, delving into the phrases commonly used when meeting and greeting others in the French language.

These phrases will help you navigate social interactions in France and other French-speaking countries, whether they are formal or casual. By learning these phrases, you will be able to introduce yourself, express friendliness, and establish connections with local people.

It's important to note that introductions in French-speaking countries not only reflect how people greet each other but also the cultural nuances that shape their social interactions and relationships.

As we explore this linguistic landscape, we will encounter phrases that capture the essence of building connections, giving us insights into the customs, habits, and attitudes surrounding introductions in French-speaking regions. Whether you are a language enthusiast, a traveler wanting to connect with locals, or simply curious about the expressions used in everyday conversations, this chapter will invite you to explore the intersection of language and social interactions.

Are you ready for this journey? Join us in this linguistic expedition as we uncover the meanings behind phrases that go beyond words, painting vivid pictures of the warm and friendly nature of introductions in the French-speaking world. From the initial "Bonjour" to sharing personal information, each phrase reflects the cultural landscapes that shape the French language.

So, get ready and come aboard as we guide you through the captivating world of introductions in French. Through the lens of language, we embark on a fascinating exploration of the phrases that bridge the gap between strangers and friends.

But before we delve into the phrases and vocabulary, here is some valuable information that will be useful to you.

Buses

Buses play a significant role in the transportation landscape of France and other French-speaking countries, offering a convenient and accessible mode of travel. These buses not only serve as a means of transportation but also provide an opportunity to engage with locals and immerse oneself in the cultural fabric of the region.

When using public transportation, such as buses, for an extended period, it's common to develop familiar relationships with bus drivers and fellow passengers. Bus drivers often recognize regular passengers and greet them warmly when they board. Additionally, striking up conversations with fellow passengers is not uncommon, as bus rides can provide a chance to connect with locals and learn more about the places you're visiting.

Buses in France and other French-speaking countries come in various shapes and sizes, reflecting the diverse urban landscapes and serving as vital transportation links for millions of residents. While some cities have organized and modern bus systems, others operate with a more informal yet effective approach. These buses traverse through different neighborhoods, suburbs, and even remote areas, providing an essential lifeline for commuters.

Bus routes are designed to adapt to the topography and layout of each city, offering passengers a window into the local life and communities they pass through. Some routes have frequent bus services, with intervals as short as three minutes, while others may have longer intervals of 15 to 40 minutes, depending on the destination. If you have questions about bus frequency, don't be afraid to ask a local, "À quelle fréquence passent les bus?" (How frequently do the buses come?)

Bus stops often serve as hubs for social interactions, where people gather and engage in conversations while waiting for their bus. These interactions allow passengers to discuss various topics, such as the city, local destinations, or even politics. The affordability and accessibility of bus fares in France and other French-speaking countries also contribute to a sense of community among passengers, fostering a warm and inclusive environment onboard.

When paying for a bus ride, it's recommended to have the exact fare ready. If paying with a banknote and the driver doesn't have enough change, you may need to wait until other passengers pay and the driver accumulates enough coins or small bills to provide change. This process can take place over the course of a few bus stops or even the entire journey from the terminal to your destination.

Metros and Subways

In addition to buses, many French-speaking cities boast efficient and extensive metro systems, offering rapid transit and connecting key destinations across sprawling urban landscapes. These metro systems serve as vital arteries in bustling metropolises like Paris, Montreal, and Brussels, contributing to the cultural and economic vibrancy of the cities they serve. Metro stations, often adorned with artwork or unique architectural features, add a touch of artistic flair to daily commutes.

Taxis and Ride-Sharing Services

Taxis and ride-sharing services like Uber or Lyft also play a crucial role in the transportation landscape of France and other French-speaking countries. Taxis, easily recognizable by their distinctive colors and signage, provide a regulated and metered fare structure. Ride-sharing services offer a modern and convenient alternative, with user-friendly interfaces and cashless payment options.

Both taxis and ride-sharing services contribute to the accessibility and efficiency of transportation, accommodating diverse preferences and enhancing the overall urban mobility experience in France and other French-speaking countries.

Common Phrases and Vocabulary

Common Phrases	Translation
What bus route takes me to …?	Quelle ligne de bus m'emmène à… ?
What metro line takes me to …?	Quelle ligne de métro m'emmène à… ?
How frequent is the bus?	Quelle est la fréquence d'arrivée du bus ?
How frequent is the train/metro?	Quelle est la fréquence du train/métro ?
How much is the bus fare?	Combien coûte le ticket du bus ?
How much is the metro fare?	Combien coûte le ticket du métro ?
How much is the train fare?	Combien coûte le ticket du train ?
How much is the taxi fare?	Quel est le tarif de la course du taxi ?
I need help.	J'ai besoin d'aide.
Where can I take the bus/metro/train/taxi?	Où puis-je prendre le bus/métro/train/taxi ?
Where can I buy a card for the bus/metro/train?	Où puis-je acheter un ticket de bus/métro/train ?
I want to add credit to my card.	Je veux ajouter du crédit à ma carte.
Where do I have to get off if I need to go to …?	Où dois-je descendre si je dois aller à … ?
What is the closest station?	Quelle est la station la plus proche ?
Where do I need to transfer?	Où dois-je faire une correspondance ?
Where can I transfer?	Où puis-je prendre une correspondance ?
What time does the bus service begin?	A quelle heure commence le service de bus ?
What time does the bus service finish?	À quelle heure se termine le service de bus ?
Could you tell me how to get to …?	Pouvez-vous me dire comment me rendre à … ?
Am I close to …?	Suis-je proche de … ?
Can I sit here?	Puis-je m'asseoir ici ?
Yes, of course!	Oui, bien sûr !
No, it is taken.	Non, c'est occupé.
Where is the hospital?	Où se trouve l'hôpital ?
I need to go to a hospital.	Je dois aller à l'hôpital.
Where is the police station?	Où se trouve le poste de police ?
Where do I exit the station?	Où puis-je sortir de la station ?
What platform do I need if I am going to …?	De quelle plateforme ai-je besoin si je veux… ?
Where can I get a map of the metro lines?	Où puis-je obtenir un plan des lignes de métro ?
Where can I get a map of the bus lines?	Où puis-je obtenir un plan des lignes de bus ?
Where is the restroom?	Où se trouvent les toilettes ?

How long does the bus take to get to …?	Combien de temps met le bus pour arriver à… ?
How long does the train take to get to …?	Combien de temps met le train pour arriver à… ?
How long does the metro take to get to …?	Combien de temps met le métro pour arriver à… ?
Can I get there by walking?	Puis-je m'y rendre à pied ?
What route is this bus?	Quelle est la ligne de ce bus ?
What line is this train?	Quelle est la ligne de ce train ?
What time is it?	Quelle heure est-il ?
What time will we arrive?	À quelle heure arriverons-nous ?
Where can I buy one ticket?	Où puis-je acheter un billet ?
Can I pay with spare money or do I need to buy a card?	Puis-je payer avec de l'argent ou dois-je acheter une carte ?
Can I buy a weekly/monthly/unlimited pass?	Puis-je acheter un abonnement hebdomadaire/mensuel/illimité ?
Is there a student discount?	Existe-t-il une réduction pour les étudiants ?
Where can I find an available taxi?	Où puis-je trouver un taxi disponible ?
Where is the taxi terminal?	Où se trouve la station des taxis ?
Where are you going?	Où allez-vous ?
What is your destination?	Quelle est votre destination ?
Please, take me to [location].	S'il vous plaît, emmenez-moi à …
I need to go to [location].	Je dois me rendre à …
How long will it take to get to [location]?	Combien de temps faut-il pour se rendre à …?
What is the fare for a trip to [location]?	Quel est le prix du trajet jusqu'à …?
Can you drive faster?	Pouvez-vous conduire plus vite ?
Can you drive slower?	Pouvez-vous conduire plus lentement ?
Can you turn up volume?	Pouvez-vous augmenter le volume ?
Can you turn down volume?	Pouvez-vous baisser le volume ?
Can you change the radio station?	Pouvez-vous changer de station de radio ?
Can you turn on the radio?	Pouvez-vous allumer la radio ?
Can you turn off the radio?	Pouvez-vous éteindre la radio ?
Is it difficult to catch a taxi in this part of the city?	Est-il difficile de prendre un taxi dans cette zone de la ville ?
There is a lot of traffic.	Il y a beaucoup de circulation.
Can I pay with a card or cash?	Puis-je payer par carte ou en espèces ?
Please, take this route.	S'il vous plaît, prenez cet itinéraire.
Please, use the GPS.	S'il vous plaît, utilisez le GPS.

Please, open the window.	S'il-vous-plaît, ouvrez la fenêtre.
Please, close the window.	S'il-vous-plaît, fermez la fenêtre.
Can you help me with my luggage?	Pouvez-vous m'aider avec mes bagages ?
Can you turn on the AC?	Pouvez-vous allumer la climatisation ?
Can you turn off the AC?	Pouvez-vous éteindre la climatisation ?
Please, open the trunk.	S'il vous plaît, ouvrez le coffre.
I'll pay with a card.	Je paierai par carte.
I'll pay with cash.	Je paierai en espèces.
You can drop me off here.	Vous pouvez me déposer ici.
You can drop me off there.	Vous pouvez me déposer là-bas.
You can drop me off in the corner.	Vous pouvez me déposer dans le coin.
I would like to go to the airport.	Je voudrais aller à l'aéroport.
I would like to go to the museum.	Je voudrais aller au musée.
I would like to go to downtown.	Je voudrais aller au centre-ville.
I would like to go to the hotel …	Je voudrais aller à l'hôtel …
I'll get off here.	Je descends ici.
I'm sorry, can you wait for me a couple of minutes?	Je suis désolé, pouvez-vous m'attendre quelques minutes ?
How long will it take to get to my destination?	Combien de temps faudra-t-il pour arriver à destination ?
How can I get to [location] from here?	Comment puis-je me rendre à … à partir d'ici ?
What time is rush hour?	Quelle est l'heure de pointe ?
Can I have your card for future trips?	Puis-je avoir votre carte pour mes prochains déplacements ?
Can you stop by the supermarket on the way back?	Pouvez-vous vous arrêter au supermarché sur le chemin du retour ?
How long have you been a driver and what places do you recommend in the city?	Depuis combien de temps êtes-vous chauffeur et quels sont les endroits que vous recommandez dans la ville ?
Is this part of the city safe?	Est-ce que cette partie de la ville est sécurisée ?
Until what time do you operate?	Jusqu'à quelle heure travaillez-vous ?
Let me know when I can get off.	Faites-moi savoir quand je peux descendre.
Do you have a phone charger?	Avez-vous un chargeur de téléphone ?
Please, take me to the downtown area.	S'il vous plaît, emmenez-moi au centre-ville.
Please, take me to the downtown bus terminal.	S'il vous plaît, emmenez-moi au terminus de bus du centre-ville.
Please, stop at the next gas station.	S'il vous plaît, arrêtez-vous à la prochaine station-service.

I can walk from here.	Je peux marcher à partir d'ici.
Thank you for bringing me home.	Merci de m'avoir ramené à la maison.
Have a nice day/evening/night.	Passez une bonne journée/soirée/nuit.

Vocabulary	Translation
Good morning!	Bonjour !
Good afternoon!	Bon après-midi !
Good evening! Good night!	Bonne soirée! Bonne nuit!
Metro/train station	Station de métro/train
Metro/train Terminal	Terminal de métro/train
Fare	Tarifa
Map	Carte
Transfers	Transferts
Departures	Départs
Arrivals	Arrivées
Schedule	Calendrier
Restroom	Salle de repos
Elevator	Ascenseur
North	Nord
South	Sud
East	Est
West	Ouest
Avenue	Avenue
Street	Rue
Boulevard	Boulevard
Cross the Street	Traverser la rue
Pedestrians' bridge	Passerelle pour piétons
Traffic light	Feu de circulation
Far	Loin
Close, near	Près de
Distance	Distance
Car	Voiture
Bicycle	Vélo
Free Admission	Entrée libre
Discount	Remise
Children's Fare	Tarif enfant

Chapter 3
Food and drinks

ood holds a special place in French and francophone cultures, where sharing meals with loved ones is a cherished tradition. Whether you're a food enthusiast or someone looking to explore the culinary landscape of France and francophone countries, we are here to help you develop the language skills necessary to confidently communicate in restaurants, order your favorite dishes, and fully immerse yourself in the delightful world of French and francophone cuisine.

In this chapter, we will cover a range of topics related to food and dining in France and francophone countries. Here's a preview of what's to come:

Building a Strong Food Vocabulary: We will provide you with a solid foundation of French and francophone food-related vocabulary, enabling you to easily identify ingredients, dishes, and flavors.

Mastering the Art of Ordering: Whether you find yourself in a traditional French bistro, a bustling market in a francophone city, or enjoying street food from a local vendor, you will learn how to confidently place orders in French and navigate menus.

Expressing Your Preferences: Discover how to confidently communicate your food preferences, allergies, and dietary restrictions, ensuring that each meal caters to your tastes and requirements.

Asking Informed Questions: Equip yourself with the ability to ask questions about the menu, ingredients, and preparation methods, allowing you to make informed choices and engage in meaningful conversations with local chefs and fellow diners.

By the end of this chapter, you will be well-prepared to savor the diverse and delicious dishes that France and francophone countries have to offer. Not only will you navigate the world of food and dining with ease, but you will also engage in meaningful conversations with locals, forging connections through the universal language of cuisine. Together, we will enhance your conversational skills and explore the tantalizing world of French and francophone food! Bon appétit!

Common Phrases	Translation
Can I have the menu, please?	Puis-je avoir le menu, s'il vous plaît ?
Do you have free tables?	Avez-vous des tables libres ?
Do you have tables by the windows/balcony?	Avez-vous des tables près des fenêtres/balcons ?
I am ready to order.	Je suis prêt pour commander.
I'd like to order.	Je souhaite commander.
Can we I have two more minutes? I'm not ready to order yet.	Pouvons-nous avoir encore deux minutes ? Je ne suis pas encore prêt pour commander.
What is the most popular dish?	Quel est le plat le plus populaire ?
What do you recommend?	Que recommandez-vous ?
What is this?	Qu'est-ce que c'est ?
Is this spicy?	Est-ce que c'est piquant ?

Can you make it spicier?	Pouvez-vous le rendre plus piquant ?
Can you make it less spicy?	Pouvez-vous le rendre moins piquant ?
I'll take this to go.	Je vais l'emporter.
Can I have a box/bag for this?	Puis-je avoir une boîte/un sac pour cela ?
Can I have the bill, please?	Puis-je avoir l'addition, s'il vous plaît ?
I'm ready to pay.	Je suis prêt à payer.
I'd like to pay.	J'aimerais payer.
Do you accept credit cards?	Acceptez-vous les cartes de crédit ?
Should I pay here at the table or at the cashier?	Dois-je payer ici, à table, ou à la caisse ?
We only accept cash.	Nous n'acceptons que l'espèce.
Tips are included in the bill.	Le pourboire est inclus dans l'addition.
Tips are voluntary.	Le pourboire est facultatif.
The food here is good.	La nourriture ici est bonne.
The meal was delicious.	Le repas était délicieux.
I'm vegetarian.	Je suis végétarien(e).
I'm vegan.	Je suis vegan(e).
I don't eat meat.	Je ne mange pas de viande.
I have allergies to…	Je suis allergique à …
I'd like to drink…	J'aimerais boire …
I would like to have some water.	Je voudrais un peu d'eau.
I'd like a cup of wine…	Je voudrais une tasse de vin...
To drink, I want a carbonated water.	Pour la boisson, je veux de l'eau gazeuse.
Can I have cold water?	Puis-je avoir de l'eau froide ?
One bottle of water, please.	Une bouteille d'eau, s'il vous plaît.
It smells good.	Ça sent bon.
Please, I need some extra sauce.	S'il vous plaît, j'ai besoin d'un peu plus de sauce.
Can you pass me the salt?	Pouvez-vous me passer le sel ?
Can you pass me the pepper?	Pouvez-vous me passer le poivre ?
What is the most popular dish?	Quel est le plat le plus populaire ?
I'd like to have a coffee.	Je voudrais un café.
I'd like to have an expresso.	Je voudrais un expresso.
I'd like to have an Americano.	Je voudrais un Americano.
How much is this?	Combien cela coûte-t-il ?
What time do you close?	À quelle heure fermez-vous ?
What time do you open?	À quelle heure ouvrez-vous ?
I want to order some dessert.	Je voudrais commander un dessert.
Can I have an extra spoon?	Puis-je avoir une cuillère supplémentaire ?

Can I have an extra fork?	Puis-je avoir une fourchette supplémentaire ?
Can I have an extra plate?	Puis-je avoir une assiette supplémentaire ?
Can I have more napkins?	Puis-je avoir d'autres serviettes ?
I'm sorry.	Je suis désolé.
Thank you so much!	Merci beaucoup !
Can you repeat that, please?	Pouvez-vous répéter cela, s'il vous plaît ?
The food is to go.	Le repas est à emporter.
I would like to make a reservation.	J'aimerais faire une réservation.
Please, pack this to go.	S'il vous plaît, emballez ça à emporter.
Do you need anything else?	Avez-vous besoin d'autre chose ?
Would you like to order anything else?	Voulez-vous commander autre chose ?
When will the food be ready?	Quand le repas sera-t-il prêt ?
You will have to wait a little longer than usual.	Vous devrez attendre un peu plus longtemps que d'habitude.
How is this dish prepared?	Comment ce plat est-il préparé ?
Does it contain…?	Contient-il… ?
White rice, please!	Du riz blanc, s'il vous plaît !
I want scrambled eggs.	Je veux des œufs brouillés.
I want scrambled eggs with ham.	Je veux des œufs brouillés avec du jambon.
I want sunny-side eggs.	Je veux des œufs au plat.
It is my first time trying this kind of food.	C'est la première fois que j'essaie ce genre de nourriture.
I'm loving it!	J'adore ça !
What types of bread do you have?	Quels sont les types de pain disponibles ?
Does it contain caffeine?	Contient-il de la caféine ?
I would like to try some street food.	J'aimerais goûter à la cuisine de rue.
Where can I order pizza?	Où puis-je commander une pizza ?
What are the healthy options?	Quels sont les options saines ?
I'd like to order a sweet dessert.	J'aimerais commander un dessert sucré.
I can't eat dairy products.	Je ne peux pas manger de produits laitiers.
Can I have a salad, please?	Puis-je avoir une salade, s'il vous plaît ?
Do you have a kids' menu?	Avez-vous un menu pour enfants ?
Please, add more cheese.	S'il vous plaît, ajoutez du fromage.
Do you have a buffet?	Avez-vous un buffet ?
Are the drinks unlimited?	Les boissons sont-elles à volonté ?
I would like to add something to my order…	Je voudrais ajouter quelque chose à ma commande…

Where is the bathroom?	Où se trouvent les toilettes ?
Where can I pay?	Où puis-je payer ?
The place is beautiful.	L'endroit est magnifique.
I'll leave a positive review!	Je laisserai un commentaire positif !
I'd definitively come back!	Je reviendrai certainement !
I'd love the service!	J'adorerais le service !

Common Vocabulary	Translation
Food	Aliments, nourriture
Breakfast	Petit-déjeuner
Lunch	Déjeuner
Dinner	Dîner
Snack	Collation, Goûter
Meat	Viande
Chicken	Poulet
Beef	Bœuf
Pork	Porc
Fish	Poisson
Vegetables	Légumes
Onion	Oignon
Carrot	Carotte
Mushroom	Champignon
Jalapeno	Jalapeno
Lettuce	Laitue
Cabbage	Chou
Tomato	Tomate
Tomato sauce	Sauce tomate
Milk	Lait
Cheese	Fromage
Cream	Crème
Butter	Beurre
Egg	Oeufs
Bread	Pain
Fruit	Fruit
Apple	Pomme
Banana	Banane
Pear	Poire

Watermelon	Pastèque
Melon	Melon
Pineapple	Anans
Strawberry	Fraise
Beans	Haricots
Rice	Riz
Pasta	Pâtes
Salt	Sel
Pepper	Poivre, Piment
Sugar	Sucre
Oil	Huile
Vinegar	Vinaigre
Garlic	Ail
Spices	Épices
Seasoning	Assaisonnement
Dressing	Dressage
Salad	Salade
Menu	Menu
Restaurant	Restaurant
Café	Café
Bakery	Boulangerie
Butchery	Boucherie
Soup	Soupe
Appetizer	Apéritif, Entrée
Main Dish	Plat principal
Dessert	Dessert
Wine	Vin
Water	Eau
Carbonated water	Eau gazeuse
Cider	Cidre
Grilled	Grillé
Baked	Au four
Steamed	À la vapeur
Well-done	Bien cuit
Half-done	Demi-cuit
Stew	Ragoût
Sushi	Sushi

Sandwich	Sandwich
Ham	Jambon
Toast	Toast, pain grillé
Spoon	Cuillère
Fork	Fourchette
Knife	Couteau
Plate	Assiette
Cup	Tasse
Napkin	Serviette de table
Glass	Verre
Cutlery	Coutellerie
Kitchen	Cuisine
Ice cream	Glace
Cake	Cake, gâteau
Hamburger	Hamburger
Typical food	Plats typiques
Street food	Aliments de rue
Bacon	Bacon, lard

Chapter 4
Making friends
(socializing)

n this chapter, we will dive into the world of socializing in French-speaking countries. Making friends and connecting with others is an essential part of any culture, and knowing the right phrases to use can make all the difference. Whether you're traveling to France or simply interested in expanding your language skills, this chapter will equip you with the necessary tools to navigate social interactions in French.

From casual greetings to engaging in small talk, we will explore the nuances and customs involved in making connections with locals. Learning these phrases will not only enhance your language skills but also enable you to immerse yourself in the vibrant social scene of French-speaking regions.

As we uncover the phrases and expressions used in social settings, you will gain valuable insights into the cultural norms and traditions that shape French interactions. By mastering these linguistic tools, you will have the confidence to initiate conversations, build relationships, and create lasting connections with people from diverse backgrounds.

So, buckle up and get ready to embark on a journey that goes beyond language learning – join us as we unravel the art of making friends in French-speaking countries. Whether you're a language enthusiast, a traveler seeking authentic experiences, or simply curious about the social dynamics of French-speaking cultures, this chapter is your gateway to understanding the power of communication in forging meaningful relationships.

Let's dive in and explore the rich tapestry of socializing in French – one conversation at a time.

Examples of phrases for making friends

Common Phrases	Translation
How are you?	Comment vas-tu ?
I'm fine, thanks. How are you?	Ça va, merci. Et toi ?
I'm fine, thanks.	Je vais bien, merci.
What is your name ?	Comment tu t'appelles ?
My name is [your name]. What about you?	Je m'appelle [your name]. Et toi ?
Nice to meet you.	Enchanté(e) / Ravi(e).
What do you do for a living?	Qu'est-ce que tu fais dans la vie ?
Where are you from?	Tu es d'où ? / D'où viens-tu ?
Do you have any siblings?	Tu as des frères et sœurs ?
Would you like to go grab a coffee together?	Tu veux aller prendre un café ensemble ?
We should meet up for a coffee sometime. Would you be up for it?	On devrait se retrouver pour un café un de ces jours. Ça te dirait ?
Of course! It would be great to meet up. Let me know when you're available.	Bien sûr ! Ce serait super de se retrouver. Tiens-moi au courant de tes disponibilités.

I love French cuisine. Do you know a good restaurant to recommend?	J'adore la cuisine française. Tu connais un bon restaurant à me recommander ?
We could meet up for dinner one of these days. What do you think?	On pourrait se retrouver pour dîner un de ces jours. Qu'est-ce que tu en penses ?
How do you like Paris so far?	Comment tu trouves Paris jusqu'à présent ?
Have you visited any interesting places in France?	Tu as déjà visité des endroits intéressants en France ?
Yes, I've been to Paris and Lyon. I loved the beauty of these cities. Have you visited France?	Oui, j'ai visité Paris et Lyon. J'ai adoré la beauté de ces villes. Et toi, as-tu visité la France ?
What do you like to do for fun?	Qu'aimes-tu faire pour t'amuser ?
Let's exchange numbers and keep in touch.	Échangeons nos numéros et restons en contact.
What are your hobbies?	Quels sont tes hobbies / loisirs ?
I enjoy sports and reading books. How about you, what are your favorite pastimes?	J'aime faire du sport et lire des livres. Et toi, quels sont tes passe-temps préférés ?
Do you have any plans for the weekend?	Tu as des plans pour ce week-end ?
Yes, I'm planning to go shopping. What about you, what are you going to do?	Oui, je prévois d'aller faire du shopping. Et toi, qu'est-ce que tu vas faire ?
Do you like French music?	Est-ce que tu aimes la musique française ?
Yes, I enjoy listening to French music, especially French songs. How about you, do you like French music?	Oui, j'aime écouter de la musique française, en particulier la chanson française. Et toi, apprécies-tu la musique française ?
Do you have any recommendations for French movies to watch?	Tu as des recommandations pour des films français à regarder ?
Yes, I recommend "Amélie" and "Intouchables". They are very interesting movies. Have you watched any French films?	Oui, je te conseille "Amélie" et "Intouchables". Ce sont des films très intéressants. Et toi, as-tu déjà regardé des films français ?

Practice conversations for talking about making friends (socializing):

To help you start conversations easily in French, you'll find in the following 20 examples of simple conversations to socialize with other people about different topics.

All you have to do is practice these dialogues and repeat them several times, to help you memorize them.

Dialogue 1: Meeting at a Coffee Shop

Person A: Hey, I've noticed you're reading the latest book by J.K. Rowling. How do you find it so far?

Person B: Oh, hi! I'm actually loving it. It's been a captivating read. How about you? Are you a fan of her work?

Person A: Salut, j'ai remarqué que tu lis le dernier livre de J.K. Rowling. Comment le trouves-tu jusqu'à présent ?

Person B: Oh, salut ! En fait, je l'adore. C'est une lecture captivante. Et toi ? Es-tu fan de son travail ?

Dialogue 2: At a Yoga Class

Person A: This was a great session, wasn't it? I feel so relaxed now.

Person B: Absolutely, it was my first time here. Do you come often?

Person A: C'était une super séance, n'est-ce pas ? Je me sens tellement détendu maintenant.

Person B: Absolument, c'était ma première fois ici. Tu viens souvent ?

Dialogue 3: Joining a Book Club Meeting

Person A: I'm new to the book club. Have you been coming here long?

Person B: Welcome! Yes, I've been part of this club for about a year. It's really fun. What book genres do you like?

Person A: Je suis nouveau dans le club de lecture. Tu viens ici depuis longtemps ?

Person B: Bienvenue ! Oui, je fais partie de ce club depuis environ un an. C'est vraiment amusant. Quels genres de livres aimes-tu ?

Dialogue 4: At a Networking Event

Person A: I've really enjoyed the talks today. What brings you to this event?

Person B: I'm actually looking to meet people in the tech industry. I'm a web developer. How about you?

Person A: J'ai vraiment apprécié les présentations aujourd'hui. Qu'est-ce qui t'amène à cet événement ?

Person B: En fait, je cherche à rencontrer des gens dans l'industrie technologique. Je suis développeur web. Et toi ?

Dialogue 5: First Meeting in a New City

Person A: How long have you been living in this city?

Person B: About three years now. It's great! Do you need some recommendations on places to visit?

Person A: Depuis combien de temps habites-tu dans cette ville ?

Person B: Depuis environ trois ans. C'est génial ! Tu as besoin de recommandations de lieux à visiter ?

Dialogue 6: Meeting Someone at a Concert

Person A: Isn't this band amazing? I've been a fan for years.

Person B: Definitely! It's my first time seeing them live. The energy is incredible!

Person A: Ce groupe n'est-il pas incroyable ? Je suis fan depuis des années.

Person B: Définitivement ! C'est la première fois que je les vois en live. L'énergie est incroyable !

Dialogue 7: During a Cooking Class

Person A: I've always wanted to learn how to make this dish. Are you enjoying the class?

Person B: Yes, it's fantastic! I love cooking. It's my first time trying this cuisine, though. How about you?

Person A: J'ai toujours voulu apprendre à faire ce plat. Tu aimes le cours ?

Person B: Oui, c'est fantastique ! J'adore cuisiner. C'est ma première fois avec cette cuisine, cependant. Et toi ?

Dialogue 8: Meeting a Neighbor

Person A: I've just moved in next door. I thought I'd come over to say hi.

Person B: Oh, welcome to the neighborhood! If you need anything or have any questions about the area, feel free to ask.

Person A: Je viens d'emménager à côté. Je pensais passer dire bonjour.

Person B: Oh, bienvenue dans le quartier ! Si tu as besoin de quelque chose ou si tu as des questions sur le quartier, n'hésite pas à demander.

Dialogue 9: At a Language Exchange Meetup

Person A: How long have you been learning Spanish?

Person B: For a few months now. I love the language! And you? Are you learning Spanish too?

Person A: Depuis combien de temps apprends-tu l'espagnol ?

Person B: Depuis quelques mois maintenant. J'adore la langue ! Et toi ? Tu apprends aussi l'espagnol ?

Dialogue 10: Joining a Sports Club

Person A: Have you been part of this club for long? I'm thinking of joining.

Person B: Yes, I've been coming here for a couple of years. It's a great way to stay active and meet people. You should definitely join!

Person A: Tu fais partie de ce club depuis longtemps ? Je pense à m'inscrire.

Person B: Oui, je viens ici depuis quelques années. C'est un excellent moyen de rester actif et de rencontrer des gens. Tu devrais définitivement t'inscrire !

Dialogue 11: At a Local Community Event

Person A: It's nice to see so many people coming together for the community. Have you attended these events before?

Person B: Yes, I try to come to these whenever I can. It's good to feel a part of something. How about you? Is this your first event?

Person A: C'est agréable de voir autant de gens se réunir pour la communauté. Tu as déjà assisté à ces événements auparavant ?

Person B: Oui, j'essaie de venir à chaque fois que je peux. C'est bien de se sentir appartenir à quelque chose. Et toi ? C'est ton premier événement ?

Dialogue 12: On a Plane

Person A: Are you heading home or starting an adventure?

Person B: I'm actually going on a vacation. Excited to explore a new place. How about you?

Person A: Tu rentres chez toi ou tu commences une aventure ?

Person B: En fait, je pars en vacances. Excité d'explorer un nouvel endroit. Et toi ?

Dialogue 13: At a Pet Park

Person A: Your dog seems to be enjoying the park. What's their name?

Person B: That's Luna! She loves it here. And who's this?

Person A: Ton chien semble apprécier le parc. Comment s'appelle-t-il ?

Person B: C'est Luna ! Elle adore cet endroit. Et qui est-ce ?

Dialogue 14: In a College Class

Person A: This class seems interesting. What's your major?

Person B: I'm studying psychology. It's fascinating. What about you?

Person A: Ce cours semble intéressant. Quelle est ta spécialité ?

Person B: J'étudie la psychologie. C'est fascinant. Et toi ?

Dialogue 15: At a Farmers' Market

Person A: Have you tried the produce from this stall before? Everything looks so fresh.

Person B: Yes, I come here every week. The apples are the best. What do you usually like to buy?

Person A: Tu as déjà essayé les produits de ce stand auparavant ? Tout a l'air si frais.

Person B: Oui, je viens ici chaque semaine. Les pommes sont les meilleures. Qu'aimes-tu acheter d'habitude ?

Dialogue 16: At a Library

Person A: I'm looking for book recommendations. What are you reading?

Person B: I'm reading a mystery novel. It's quite gripping. What genres do you like?

Person A: Je cherche des recommandations de livres. Qu'est-ce que tu lis ?

Person B: Je lis un roman policier. C'est assez captivant. Quels genres aimes-tu ?

Dialogue 17: At a volunteer event

Person A: It's great to see so many people volunteering. What motivated you to join?

Person B: I wanted to give back to the community. And it's a great way to meet like-minded people. What about you?

Person A: C'est génial de voir autant de personnes se porter volontaires. Qu'est-ce qui t'a motivé à rejoindre ?

Person B: Je voulais redonner à la communauté. Et c'est un excellent moyen de rencontrer des personnes partageant les mêmes idées. Et toi ?

Dialogue 18: At a museum

Person A: This exhibit is incredible, isn't it?

Person B: Absolutely! Art history has always fascinated me. Do you come to museums often?

Person A: Cette exposition est incroyable, n'est-ce pas ?

Person B: Absolument ! L'histoire de l'art m'a toujours fasciné. Tu viens souvent dans les musées ?

Dialogue 19: During a hiking trip

Person A: The view from here is breathtaking. Do you hike often?

Person B: Yep, it's one of my hobbies. Nothing beats the feeling of reaching the top. You?

Person A: La vue d'ici est à couper le souffle. Tu fais souvent de la randonnée ?

Person B: Oui, c'est l'un de mes passe-temps. Rien ne vaut la sensation d'atteindre le sommet. Et toi ?

Dialogue 20: At a co-working space

Person A: I love the energy of this place. Do you work here regularly?

Person B: I do. It's a great environment for creativity. What brings you here?

Person A: J'adore l'énergie de cet endroit. Tu travailles ici régulièrement ?

Person B: Oui. C'est un excellent environnement pour la créativité. Qu'est-ce qui t'amène ici ?

Cultural tips on socializing and making friends in French speaking countries

Socializing in French-speaking countries often involves certain cultural norms and expectations. Here are some tips to help you navigate social interactions more effectively:

1. Embracing "la bise": In France, a customary way to greet both friends and acquaintances is with a kiss on the cheek known as "la bise." The number of kisses exchanged can vary by region, so observe and follow the local customs.

2. Dining traditions: Sharing a meal is a significant aspect of French socializing. Inviting someone to dine together is a common way to deepen relationships. Take the opportunity to savor delicious cuisine while getting to know your new friends.

3. Politeness and formality: French people value politeness and formality in social interactions. Remember to use phrases like "s'il vous plaît" (please) and "merci" (thank you) to show respect and appreciation.

4. Building personal connections: French culture places importance on establishing meaningful relationships. Take the time to engage in conversations and learn more about the person you are getting to know. Showing genuine interest in their interests and experiences will help you forge lasting friendships.

5. Cultural topics: Discussing cultural subjects such as art, literature, and cuisine can be a gateway to connecting with French speakers. Show your appreciation for their culture by engaging in conversations about these enriching topics.

Mastering the art of making friends and socializing in French-speaking countries is a rewarding experience that opens doors to new friendships and cultural exploration. By utilizing the language skills and cultural tips provided in this chapter, you will be well-equipped to navigate social interactions with confidence and grace. Embrace the opportunity to connect with others, learn from their experiences, and build lasting relationships that enrich your language learning journey.

Bonne chance dans votre quête d'amitié et de socialisation en français! (Good luck in your quest for friendship and socializing in French!)

Chapter 5
Talking about the Weather

Weather is a topic that is often used as a conversation starter in many cultures, including French-speaking ones. In this chapter, we will explore how to talk about the weather in French, providing you with the necessary vocabulary and phrases to engage in small talk and casual conversations with native speakers.

The weather plays a central role in daily life and can be a useful tool for connecting with others. Whether you are making polite conversation with a stranger or catching up with a friend, being able to discuss the weather is a valuable skill to have in your language arsenal.

From discussing the temperature and weather conditions to expressing your feelings about the climate, we will guide you through the key phrases and expressions used when talking about the weather in French. By mastering this chapter, you will not only be able to participate in everyday conversations but also gain a deeper understanding of cultural norms and social interactions in French-speaking countries.

So, buckle up and get ready to dive into the world of weather-related conversations in French. By the end of this chapter, you will be prepared to not only discuss the weather, but also engage in meaningful exchanges that go beyond surface-level chatter. Let's embark on this linguistic journey together and discover the hidden nuances of discussing the weather in French.

Vocabulary related to weather conditions

Common phrases	Translation
Temperature	Température
Sunny	Ensoleillé
Cloudy	Nuageux
Rainy	Pluvieux
Snowy	Neigeux
Windy	Venteux
Stormy	Orageux
Hot	Chaud
Warm	Chaud (température douce)
Cold	Froid
Hail	Grêle
Thunderstorm	Orage
Hurricane	Ouragan
Tornado	Tornade
Snowstorm	Tempête de neige
Breezy	Brise

Chilly	Frais
Humid	Humide
Freezing	Gelé
Icy	Glacial
Flurries	Flocons (de neige)
Chopping	Chaud et humide
Light rain	Pluie légère
Heavy rain	Pluie forte
High pressure	Haute pression
Low pressure	Basse pression
Fall/Autumn	Automne
Winter	Hiver
Spring	Printemps
Summer	Été
Temperature drop	Baisse de température
Weather conditions	Conditions météorologiques
Sunny day	Journée ensoleillée
Cloudy with a chance of rain	Nuageux avec risque de pluie
Snow showers expected	Chutes de neige prévues
Strong winds gusting up to 40 mph	Vents forts soufflant jusqu'à 40 km/h
Tropical storm warning in effect	Avertissement de tempête tropicale en vigueur
Dense fog advisory in the area	Avis de brouillard dense dans la région
Heat wave hitting the region	Vague de chaleur frappant la région
Sub-zero temperatures forecasted	Températures sous zéro prévues
Scattered thunderstorms expected	Orages dispersés prévus
Hail and sleet showers possible	Possibilité de grêle et de grésil
High UV index warning	Avertissement de fort indice UV
Localized downpours causing flooding	Averses localisées causant des inondations
Blowing snow reducing visibility	Chutes de neige soufflée réduisant la visibilité
Cold front moving through the area	Front froid traversant la région
Warm front bringing milder temperatures	Front chaud apportant des températures plus douces
Frost advisory overnight	Avis de gelée nocturne
Wet weather ahead	Temps humide à venir
Sweltering heat wave continues	Vague de chaleur suffocante se poursuit
Occasional showers with breaks of sun	Averse intermittente avec éclaircies
Persistent rain showers lasting all day	Averses persistantes toute la journée

Gradual clearing expected in the afternoon	Éclaircies progressives prévues dans l'après-midi
Intense thunderstorm activity approaching	Activité d'orage intense en approche
Light breeze with a mix of sun and clouds	Légère brise avec un mélange de soleil et de nuages
Humid conditions making it feel hotter	Conditions humides donnant l'impression qu'il fait plus chaud
Frost and ice forming overnight	Gel et glace se formant durant la nuit
Dry and hot weather leading to fire danger	Temps sec et chaud entraînant un danger d'incendie
Unsettled weather pattern with scattered showers	Modèle météorologique instable avec des averses dispersées
Bright and clear skies with a crisp breeze	Ciel lumineux et dégagé avec une brise fraîche
Heavy snowfall warning for the mountains	Avertissement de fortes chutes de neige dans les montagnes
Sudden temperature drop expected tonight	Baisse soudaine de température prévue cette nuit
Widespread fog causing travel delays	Brouillard généralisé causant des retards de voyage
Chilly mornings followed by warm afternoons	Matins frais suivis d'après-midis chauds
Sudden thunderstorm passing through the region	Orage soudain traversant la région
Tornado damage reported in nearby town	Dommages de tornade signalés dans une ville voisine
Heavy downpours causing flooding in low-lying areas	Fortes averses causant des inondations dans les zones basses
No relief from the heatwave in sight	Pas de répit en vue de la vague de chaleur
Violent wind gusts toppling trees	Rafales de vent violent renversant des arbres
Severe thunderstorm warning issued	Avertissement de violent orage émis
Snow drifts blocking roads in the mountains	Amas de neige bloquant les routes dans les montagnes

Practice conversations for talking about the weather

To help you start conversations about the weather easily in French, you'll find below 20 examples of small weather-related conversations to use whenever the opportunity arises.

Conversation 1:

Person A: How's the weather looking for our trip this weekend?

Person B: It's supposed to be sunny and warm.

Person A: Comment s'annonce la météo pour notre voyage ce week-end ?

Person B: Il est censé faire ensoleillé et chaud.

Conversation 2:

Person A: I heard there's a storm coming. Is it going to be windy too?

Person B: Yes, it's expected to be very windy.

Person A: J'ai entendu dire qu'une tempête arrive. Est-ce qu'il y aura du vent aussi ?

Person B: Oui, on prévoit beaucoup de vent.

Conversation 3:

Person A: I can't believe it's still snowing in April!

Person B: I know, it's been a long winter.

Person A: Je n'arrive pas à croire qu'il neige encore en avril !

Person B: Je sais, c'a été un long hiver.

Conversation 4:

Person A: What's the forecast for tomorrow?

Person B: It says there might be some scattered showers.

Person A: Quelle est la prévision pour demain ?

Person B: Ça dit qu'il pourrait y avoir quelques averses.

Conversation 5:

Person A: I love the sound of rain on the roof, don't you?

Person B: It's very soothing, especially when I'm trying to sleep.

Person A: J'adore le bruit de la pluie sur le toit, et toi ?

Person B: C'est très apaisant, surtout quand j'essaie de dormir.

Conversation 6:

Person A: Have you ever experienced a heatwave like this before?

Person B: Not this intense, it's really sweltering out there.

Person A: As-tu déjà vécu une canicule comme celle-ci auparavant ?

Person B: Pas aussi intense, il fait vraiment étouffant dehors.

Conversation 7:

Person A: I wish it would stop drizzling so we can go for a walk.

Person B: Let's wait a little longer, it might clear up soon.

Person A: J'aimerais que ça arrête de bruiner pour que nous puissions aller nous promener.

Person B: Attendons un peu plus longtemps, ça pourrait s'éclaircir bientôt.

Conversation 8:

Person A: The fog is so thick this morning, I can barely see anything.

Person B: Drive carefully, visibility is really low in these conditions.

Person A: Le brouillard est si épais ce matin, je ne peux presque rien voir.

Person B: Conduis prudemment, la visibilité est vraiment faible dans ces conditions.

Conversation 9:

Person A: Do you think the snow will accumulate enough for a snowman?

Person B: It's possible, the weather report mentioned heavy snowfall.

Person A: Penses-tu que la neige va s'accumuler suffisamment pour faire un bonhomme de neige ?

Person B: C'est possible, le bulletin météo mentionnait des chutes de neige abondantes.

Conversation 10:

Person A: I hope the thunderstorm doesn't cause any power outages.

Person B: We should prepare just in case, it looks like a strong one.

Person A: J'espère que l'orage ne provoquera pas de pannes de courant.

Person B: Nous devrions nous préparer au cas où, cela semble être un fort orage.

Conversation 11:

Person A: It's so muggy today, I can feel the humidity in the air.

Person B: Yes, it's really uncomfortable, I wish it would cool down.

Person A: Il fait tellement lourd aujourd'hui, je sens l'humidité dans l'air.

Person B: Oui, c'est vraiment inconfortable, j'espère que ça va se rafraîchir.

Conversation 12:

Person A: I love how the leaves change color in the fall.

Person B: Yes, the autumn foliage is really beautiful.

Person A: J'adore comment les feuilles changent de couleur en automne.

Person B: Oui, le feuillage d'automne est vraiment magnifique.

Conversation 13:

Person A: Is it going to be clear skies for the outdoor concert tonight?

Person B: According to the forecast, there won't be a single cloud.

Person A: Est-ce que le ciel sera dégagé pour le concert en plein air ce soir ?

Person B: Selon la prévision, il n'y aura pas un seul nuage.

Conversation 14:

Person A: The hail during the storm was so loud, it sounded like drumbeats.

Person B: Yes, it was quite intense, I hope it didn't damage anything.

Person A: La grêle pendant l'orage était si bruyante, on aurait dit des tambours.

Person B: Oui, c'était assez intense, j'espère que ça n'a rien endommagé.

Conversation 15:

Person A: I find the sound of crickets on a summer night so peaceful.

Person B: It's like nature's lullaby, isn't it?

Person A: Je trouve le bruit des grillons un soir d'été si paisible.

Person B: C'est comme une berceuse de la nature, n'est-ce pas ?

Conversation 16:

Person A: I love the smell of fresh rain on the grass, it's so invigorating.

Person B: It's one of my favorite scents too, it feels rejuvenating.

Person A: J'adore l'odeur de la pluie fraîche sur l'herbe, c'est si revigorant.

Person B: C'est aussi l'une de mes odeurs préférées, ça donne l'impression d'être rajeuni.

Conversation 17:

Person A: The weather forecast predicts a frost tonight.

Person B: We better cover the delicate plants in the garden.

Person A: La météo prévoit du gel cette nuit.

Person B: Nous ferions mieux de protéger les plantes délicates dans le jardin.

Conversation 18:

Person A: I hope the sun comes out soon, I miss the warmth on my skin.

Person B: Yes, it's been cloudy for too long.

Person A: J'espère que le soleil va bientôt se montrer, ça me manque cette chaleur sur ma peau.

Person B: Oui, ça fait trop longtemps qu'il fait nuageux.

Conversation 19:

Person A: The weather has been so unpredictable lately.

Person B: It's hard to plan anything with these constant changes.

Person A: La météo a été tellement imprévisible ces derniers temps.

Person B: C'est difficile de prévoir quoi que ce soit avec ces changements constants.

Conversation 20:

Person A: I love watching the lightning during a thunderstorm, it's so mesmerizing.

Person B: It's both beautiful and awe-inspiring, but also a bit scary.

Person A: J'adore regarder les éclairs pendant un orage, c'est tellement captivant.

Person B: C'est à la fois beau et impressionnant, mais aussi un peu effrayant.

Chapter 6
Accommodation, Hotels and Airbnb

s we continue our journey through the French language, let us now turn our attention to the topic of accommodation, hotels, and Airbnb. In this chapter, we will explore the essential words and phrases that will help you navigate the world of hospitality in French-speaking countries.

From booking a room to checking in and out, knowing the right vocabulary will make your stay much more enjoyable and convenient. Whether you prefer the comfort of a hotel or the coziness of an Airbnb, understanding the language of accommodation will enhance your travel experience and help you feel more at home in a foreign country.

In this chapter, we will delve into the terminology commonly used in hotels and Airbnb rentals, as well as the etiquette and customs that are important to keep in mind when staying in accommodation in French-speaking regions. By familiarizing yourself with these phrases, you will be better equipped to communicate your needs and preferences, ensuring a pleasant and stress-free stay.

So, sit back, relax, and let's embark on a linguistic exploration of accommodation in French. From "je voudrais réserver une chambre" to "où se trouve la réception," we will equip you with the language skills needed to make your stay a memorable one. Get ready to immerse yourself in the world of hotels, Airbnb, and hospitality in the French-speaking world.

Common Phrases	Translation
May I have the name for the reservation?	Puis-je avoir le nom pour la réservation ?
My reservation is for [Your Name].	Ma réservation est pour [Your Name].
I'm here to check in.	Je suis là pour m'inscrire.
I'm here to check out.	Je suis ici pour faire le point.
What time is the check in?	Quelle est l'heure d'arrivée ?
What time is the check out?	Quelle est l'heure de départ ?
Can I have an early check in?	Puis-je arriver plus tôt ?
Can I check out early?	Puis-je partir plus tôt ?
Can I have a late check out?	Est-il possible de partir plus tard ?
Please, confirm my reservation.	Je vous prie de confirmer ma réservation.
Can I pay with a debit card?	Puis-je payer avec une carte de débit ?
Can I pay with my credit card miles?	Puis-je payer avec les miles de ma carte de crédit ?
Can I pay with my credit card points?	Puis-je payer avec les points de ma carte de crédit ?
What documents do you need?	Quels sont les documents dont vous avez besoin ?
Can I have my documents back?	Puis-je récupérer mes documents ?
Here you have my passport.	Voici mon passeport.
Do you have room service?	Avez-vous un service d'étage ?

Is there room service every day?	Y a-t-il un service d'étage tous les jours ?
What is my room number?	Quel est le numéro de ma chambre ?
Here you have your room key.	Ici, vous avez la clé de votre chambre.
Can I have more than one key?	Puis-je avoir plus d'une clé ?
What is the Wi-Fi password?	Quel est le mot de passe du Wi-Fi ?
Is breakfast included?	Le petit-déjeuner est-il inclus ?
I would like to get more towels.	J'aimerais avoir plus de serviettes.
I need more towels.	J'ai besoin de plus de serviettes.
How often do you change the bedding?	À quelle fréquence changez-vous la literie ?
I need to change the bedding, please.	J'ai besoin de changer la literie, s'il vous plaît.
How do I turn on the air conditioning?	Comment allumer l'air conditionné ?
How do I turn on the heating?	Comment allumer le chauffage ?
How do I use the remote control for the AC?	Comment utiliser la télécommande de la climatisation ?
How do I use the remote control for the TV?	Comment utiliser la télécommande de la télévision ?
The remote control needs batteries.	La télécommande a besoin de piles.
Can you show me how to use the shower?	Pouvez-vous me montrer comment utiliser la douche ?
Can I keep the windows open?	Puis-je garder les fenêtres ouvertes ?
My room is too hot.	Ma chambre est trop chaude.
My room is too cold.	Ma chambre est trop froide.
How do I use the telephone in my room?	Comment utiliser le téléphone dans ma chambre ?
Can I make domestic calls free of charge?	Puis-je effectuer des appels nationaux gratuitement ?
What is the charge for international calls?	Quel est le coût des appels internationaux ?
What is the desk number?	Quel est le numéro du bureau ?
Is there a kitchen?	Y a-t-il une cuisine ?
Is there a refrigerator?	Y a-t-il un réfrigérateur ?
Are there hangers in the closet?	Y a-t-il des cintres dans le placard ?
Is there a hairdryer?	Y a-t-il un sèche-cheveux ?
Is there a mirror?	Y a-t-il un miroir ?
What are the breakfast hours?	Quels sont les horaires du petit-déjeuner ?
Breakfast service is from 7 a.m. to 10 a.m.	Le petit-déjeuner est servi de 7 heures à 10 heures.
Where are the restaurants nearby?	Où se trouvent les restaurants à proximité ?

What public transportation options are available to major tourist attractions nearby?	Quelles sont les possibilités de transport public vers les attractions touristiques principales situées à proximité ?
How close is the bus station?	À quelle distance se trouve la gare routière ?
How close is the metro station?	À quelle distance se trouve la station de métro ?
How much is the bus fare?	Quel est le prix du billet de bus ?
How do I contact you in case of emergency?	Comment puis-je vous contacter en cas d'urgence ?
How do I get to the [destination] from this hotel?	Comment puis-je me rendre à [destination] depuis cet hôtel ?
Where is the nearest ATM?	Où se trouve le distributeur de billets le plus proche ?
Can I pay with cash?	Puis-je payer en espèces ?
Do you accept credit cards?	Acceptez-vous les cartes de crédit ?
When does the swimming pool open?	À quelle heure la piscine ouvre-t-elle ?
When does the restaurant open?	À quelle heure le restaurant ouvre-t-il ?
When does the bar open?	À quelle heure le bar ouvre-t-il ?
When does the museum open?	À quelle heure le musée ouvre-t-il ses portes ?
How much is the parking fee?	Quel est le tarif de stationnement ?
Can I park in the area?	Puis-je me garer dans le quartier ?
Can I log into my streaming service accounts?	Puis-je me connecter à mes comptes de services de streaming ?
When is room cleaning done during my stay?	A quel moment le ménage des chambres est-il terminé pendant mon séjour?
Is there a coffee machine in the room?	Y a-t-il une machine à café dans la chambre ?
Can I have food from restaurants delivered to my room through room service?	Puis-je me faire livrer des plats de restaurants dans ma chambre par le service d'étage ?
Do you have tourist brochures?	Avez-vous des brochures touristiques ?
What guided tour do you recommend?	Quelle visite guidée recommandez-vous ?
Where is the elevator?	Où se trouve l'ascenseur ?
Where is the emergency exit?	Où se trouve la sortie de secours ?
I do not need more towels.	Je n'ai pas besoin de plus de serviettes.
Can I smoke in the hotel?	Puis-je fumer dans l'hôtel ?
Where are the designated smoking areas?	Où se trouvent les zones réservées aux fumeurs ?
I would like to add more days to my reservation.	Je souhaite ajouter des jours à ma réservation.
I would like to modify my reservation.	Je souhaite modifier ma réservation.
I'd like to make a dinner reservation.	J'aimerais réserver un dîner.

What are some places worth visiting in the area?	Quels sont les endroits à visiter dans la région ?
Can you call me a taxi?	Pouvez-vous m'appeler un taxi ?
Do you work directly with a taxi company?	Travaillez-vous directement avec une compagnie de taxis ?
Where is the largest shopping mall?	Où se trouve le plus grand centre commercial ?
What are the room amenities?	Quels sont les équipements de la chambre ?
Do you provide barbecue facilities?	Fournissez-vous des installations de barbecue ?
Do you have a conference room?	Disposez-vous d'une salle de conférence ?
How reliable is the Internet?	Quelle est la fiabilité de l'Internet ?
How fast is the Internet?	Quelle est la rapidité de l'Internet ?
Where are the good places for a stroll nearby?	Quels sont les bons endroits pour se promener dans les environs ?
Does this hotel/Airbnb have activities for children?	Cet hôtel/Airbnb propose-t-il des activités pour les enfants ?
Where are the art galleries or museums nearby?	Où se trouvent les galeries d'art ou les musées à proximité ?
Is there a safe in the room?	Y a-t-il un coffre-fort dans la chambre ?
What type of complementary breakfast do you offer?	Quel type de petit-déjeuner complémentaire proposez-vous ?
Can I request a different breakfast if I want to?	Puis-je demander un autre petit-déjeuner si je le souhaite ?
What is the most famous restaurant in the city?	Quel est le restaurant le plus célèbre de la ville ?
What is the most famous museum in the city?	Quel est le musée le plus célèbre de la ville ?
Do you offer spa services?	Proposez-vous des services de spa ?
Do you have a sauna?	Disposez-vous d'un sauna ?
What is the closest park?	Quel est le parc le plus proche ?
What is the closest café?	Quel est le café le plus proche ?
Where is the closest Starbucks?	Où se trouve le Starbucks le plus proche ?
Is the city bike-friendly?	La ville est-elle adaptée aux vélos ?
Where can I rent a bike?	Où puis-je louer un vélo ?
Where can I rent a scooter?	Où puis-je louer un scooter ?
Where can I rent a car?	Où puis-je louer une voiture ?
How do I get to the beach?	Comment aller à la plage ?
How do I get to the lake?	Comment se rendre au lac ?
Does this hotel/Airbnb provide facilities for people with disabilities?	Cet hôtel/Airbnb propose-t-il des facilités pour les personnes handicapées ?

Does this hotel/Airbnb offer ski equipment rental services?	Cet hôtel/Airbnb propose-t-il des services de location de matériel de ski ?
Where is the golf course nearby?	Où se trouve le terrain de golf à proximité ?
Where is the souvenir shop?	Où se trouve la boutique de souvenirs ?
Do you have a souvenir shop in the hotel?	L'hôtel dispose-t-il d'une boutique de souvenirs ?
What is the price range for the souvenirs in the shops?	Quel est le prix des souvenirs proposés dans les boutiques ?
Where can I hire an airport shuttle?	Où puis-je réserver une navette pour l'aéroport ?
Do you offer a shuttle service?	Proposez-vous un service de navette ?
Is the airport shuttle service free?	Le service de navette aéroport est-il gratuit ?
Where do locals go?	Où vont les locaux ?
Where do locals eat?	Où mangent les locaux ?
What do locals do on the weekends?	Que font les locaux le week-end ?
What is the snowboard equipment rental fee?	Quel est le tarif de location du matériel de snowboard ?
What is the surf equipment rental fee?	Quel est le tarif de location du matériel de surf ?
What is the outdoor equipment rental fee?	Quel est le tarif de location du matériel de plein air ?
Where are the cultural centers or art spaces nearby?	Où se trouvent les centres culturels ou les espaces d'art à proximité ?
Does this hotel/Airbnb provide complementary water bottles?	Cet hôtel/Airbnb fournit-il des bouteilles d'eau gratuites ?

Vocabulary	**Translation**
Hotel Airbnb	Hôtel Airbnb
Reservation	Réservation
Check-in	Arrivée
Check-out	Départ
Room	Chambre
Room number	Numéro de la chambre
Bed	Lit
Window	Fenêtre
Toilet	Toilette
Shower	Douche
Sink	Evier
Towel	Serviette
Hand towel	Serviette de toilette
Bathing robe	Peignoir de bain

Fridge	Réfrigérateur
Mini fridge	Mini-réfrigérateur
Kitchen	Cuisine
Internet	Internet
Internet password	Mot de passe Internet
Breakfast	Petit déjeuner
Breakfast included	Petit déjeuner inclus
Breakfast time	Heure du petit-déjeuner
Room service	Service de chambre
Parking	Parking
Parking included	Parking inclus
Parking fee	Parking payant
Lobby	Hall d'entrée
Elevator	Ascenseur
Smoking allowed area	Zone fumeurs
Non-smoking area	Zone non fumeur
Pool	Piscine
Gym	Gymnase
Sauna	Sauna
Balcony	Balcon
TV	TÉLÉVISION
Remote control	Télécommande
Coffee machine	Machine à café
Bottled water	Eau en bouteille
Soap	Savon
Hand soap	Savon à main
Shampoo	Shampoing
Conditioner	Après-shampoing
Slippers	Chaussons
Credit card	Carte de crédit
Cash	Argent liquide
Sofa	Canapé
Safe	Coffre-fort
Bar	Bar
Playground	Aire de jeux
Minibar	Minibar
Curtains	Rideaux

Noise	Bruit
Noise-cancelling Windows	Fenêtres antibruit
Hairdryer	Sèche-cheveux
Extra towels	Serviettes supplémentaires
Restaurant	Restaurant
Desk number	Numéro de bureau
24-hour service	Service 24 heures sur 24

Chapter 7
The Shopping Experience in French-Speaking Countries

In France and other French-speaking countries, the shopping experience is not just about purchasing goods; it's a social ritual embedded in the culture. From browsing the charming boutiques in Paris, Montreal, or Marrakech to exploring the bustling markets of Casablanca, Dakar, or Brussels, shopping is a way to connect with locals and immerse yourself in the vibrant atmosphere of the city.

Whether you're a fashionista seeking the latest trends or a collector looking for unique finds, there's something for everyone in the diverse shopping scenes of French-speaking countries. This chapter is designed to help you navigate the social aspect of shopping, from greeting shopkeepers with a warm "Bonjour" to engaging in friendly conversations with fellow shoppers.

Learn how to inquire about product details, sizes, and prices in French, negotiate and haggle like a pro, express your preferences with cultural sensitivity, and make informed decisions when making purchases. Whether you're looking for high-end fashion in Paris, traditional crafts in Morocco, or trendy finds in Montreal, our guide will empower you to socialize confidently and make the most of your shopping experiences in French-speaking regions.

Common Phrases	Translation
How much is it?	Combien cela coûte-t-il ?/Quel est son prix ?
What is the price?	Quel est le prix ?
Does it have a discount?	Y a-t-il une réduction ?
Can you give me a discount?	Pouvez-vous me faire une réduction ?
Do you have this in a different color?	Ce produit existe-t-il dans une autre couleur ?
Do you have this in a different size?	Ce produit existe-t-il dans une autre taille ?
Can I pay with cash?	Puis-je payer en espèces ?
Can I pay with credit card?	Puis-je payer par carte de crédit ?
Can I pay with my credit card point?	Puis-je payer avec les points de ma carte de crédit ?
Can I pay with my credit card miles?	Puis-je payer avec mes miles de carte de crédit ?
Do you offer loyalty reward points?	Offrez-vous des points de fidélité ?
Here you have your receipt.	Voici votre ticket de caisse.
Here you have your product.	Voici votre produit.
Do you need a bag?	Avez-vous besoin d'un sac ?
Is this the final price?	Est-ce le prix final ?
Does the price include taxes?	Le prix inclut-il les taxes ?
The price does not include taxes.	Le prix n'inclut pas les taxes.
Is there a discount for bulk purchases?	Existe-t-il une réduction pour les achats en gros ?
I need a receipt, please.	J'ai besoin d'un reçu, s'il vous plaît.
Can I try it?	Puis-je l'essayer ?

Can I try in on?	Puis-je faire un essai ?
Where is the fitting room?	Où se trouve la cabine d'essayage ?
Do you have this in a bigger size?	Avez-vous cette taille en plus grand ?
Do you have this in a smaller size?	Est-ce que vous l'avez dans une taille plus petite ?
Do you accept returns?	Acceptez-vous les retours ?
What is the return policy?	Quelle est la politique de retour ?
We do not accept returns.	Nous n'acceptons pas les retours.
We accept returns if the product still has the tags.	Nous acceptons les retours si le produit a encore ses étiquettes.
How long is the sale going on?	Combien de temps durent les soldes ?
How long will the discount last?	Quelle est la durée de la réduction ?
What is the most popular brand?	Quelle est la marque la plus populaire ?
What is the most popular product?	Quel est le produit le plus populaire ?
What material is it made of?	En quelle matière est-il fabriqué ?
It is made of synthetic material.	Il est en matière synthétique.
It is made of leather.	Il est en cuir.
It is made of denim.	Il est en denim.
I like this handbag.	J'aime ce sac à main.
I like those shoes.	J'aime ces chaussures.
I don't like the wallet.	Je n'aime pas ce portefeuille.
I don't like these pants.	Je n'aime pas ce pantalon.
Does the product have warranty?	Le produit a-t-il une garantie ?
How long does the warranty last?	Quelle est la durée de la garantie ?
Can I see it?	Puis-je le voir ?
Can you show that product over there?	Pouvez-vous montrer ce produit là-bas ?
You can see it.	Vous pouvez le voir.
You can try it.	Vous pouvez l'essayer.
It is not for sale.	Il n'est pas à vendre.
Is it for sale?	Est-il en vente ?
What is the lowest price?	Quel est le prix le plus bas ?
What is the best price you can offer?	Quel est le meilleur prix que vous puissiez offrir ?
Can I find this product in other stores?	Puis-je trouver ce produit dans d'autres magasins ?
It is an exclusive product.	Il s'agit d'un produit exclusif.
It is not available in other stores.	Il n'est pas disponible dans d'autres magasins.
This is a perfect gift.	C'est un cadeau parfait.
It is a unique gift.	C'est un cadeau unique.

What do you recommend?	Que recommandez-vous ?
What time does the shop open?	Quelle est l'heure d'ouverture du magasin ?
What time does the shop close?	À quelle heure le magasin ferme-t-il ?
Is it open during the weekends?	Est-il ouvert le week-end ?
This is the best price.	C'est le meilleur prix.
It is a reasonable price.	C'est un prix raisonnable.
You will not find a better price.	Vous ne trouverez pas de meilleur prix.
It is really beautiful.	C'est vraiment beau.
It is really special.	Il est vraiment spécial.
It represents our culture.	Cela représente notre culture.
It is a traditional dress.	C'est une robe traditionnelle.
It is a traditional hat.	C'est un chapeau traditionnel.
Can you ship it to my country?	Pouvez-vous l'expédier dans mon pays ?
How much is the shipping to my country?	Quel est le coût de l'expédition dans mon pays ?
What is the weight of this?	Quel est le poids de ce chapeau ?
Where is this made?	Où est-il fabriqué ?
How do I have to take care of it?	Comment dois-je l'entretenir ?
Can I see it first?	Puis-je le voir d'abord ?
Can I open the package?	Puis-je ouvrir le paquet ?
You cannot open the package, but I have a product sample.	Vous ne pouvez pas ouvrir l'emballage, mais j'ai un échantillon du produit.
What type of sounds does it make?	Quel type de sons produit-il ?
Does it have special features?	A-t-il des caractéristiques particulières ?
Is this a new product?	S'agit-il d'un nouveau produit ?
Can you wrap it as a present?	Pouvez-vous l'emballer comme cadeau ?
Does it have an additional cost?	Y a-t-il un coût supplémentaire ?
I can wrap it as a present with no additional cost.	Je peux l'emballer comme cadeau sans coût supplémentaire.
Do you accept discount coupons?	Acceptez-vous les bons de réduction ?
Can I have a better price if I buy more than one?	Puis-je bénéficier d'un meilleur prix si j'en achète plusieurs ?
How long does the shipping take?	Combien de temps dure l'expédition ?
Is it available online?	Est-il disponible en ligne ?
Is it sold on the Internet?	Est-il vendu sur Internet ?
Is it safe for kids?	Le produit est-il sans danger pour les enfants ?
The product is for 3-year-old kids or older.	Le produit est destiné aux enfants de 3 ans ou plus.
The product is not safe for kids.	Le produit n'est pas sûr pour les enfants.

It is not a safe product for carry-on luggage.	Ce n'est pas un produit sûr pour les bagages à main.
Is there any type of allergic reaction?	Y a-t-il un risque de réaction allergique ?
What type of warranty does the product have?	Quel type de garantie le produit offre-t-il ?
What type of warranty do you offer?	Quel type de garantie offrez-vous ?
Can it be customized?	Peut-on le personnaliser ?
Can my name be engraved?	Mon nom peut-il être gravé ?
What is the return policy?	Quelle est la politique de retour ?
Can I pay with dollars?	Puis-je payer en dollars ?
Can I pay with the local currency?	Puis-je payer avec la monnaie locale ?
Are taxes included?	Les taxes sont-elles incluses ?
Is this the final price?	S'agit-il du prix final ?
The best store in the city is…	Le meilleur magasin de la ville est…
The best shopping mall in the city is…	Le meilleur centre commercial de la ville est…
How do you use it?	Comment l'utilise-t-on ?
How do you eat it?	Comment peut-on le manger ?
The telephone price is…	Le prix du téléphone est de…
The book price is…	Le prix du livre est de…
It has special features.	Il a des caractéristiques particulières.
It is a traditional product.	C'est un produit traditionnel.
This is the best store in the country.	C'est le meilleur magasin du pays.
This is the most exclusive product we have.	C'est le produit le plus exclusif que nous ayons.
Add it to my bill.	Veuillez l'ajouter à ma facture.
I won't buy it.	Je ne l'achèterai pas.
I don't need it.	Je n'en ai pas besoin.
I'll pick it up tomorrow.	Je passerai le prendre demain.

Common Vocabulary	Translation
Shopping	Shopping
Store	Magasins
Shopping mall	Centre commercial
Market	Marché
Open-air market	Marché de plein air
Supermarket	Supermarché
Product	Produit
Price	Prix
Package	Emballage

Box	Boîte
Tag	Étiquette
Sell	Vendre
Transaction	Transaction
Payment	Paiement
Pay with cash	Payer en espèces
Pay with card	Paiement par carte
Receipt	Reçu
Reimbursement	Remboursement
Warranty	Garantie
Size	Taille
Color	Couleur
Shape	Forme
Brand	Marque
Style	Style
Origin	Origine
Model	Modèle
Manufacturing date	Date de fabrication
Manufacturing place	Lieu de fabrication
Expiration date	Date de péremption
To try something on	Essayer quelque chose
Features	Caractéristiques
Special features	Caractéristiques spéciales
Material	Matériau
Fabric	Tissu
Denim	Denim
Polyester	Polyester
Synthetic	Synthétique
Leather	Cuir
Wool	Laine
Seller	Vendeur
Consumer	Consommateur
Event	Evénement
Coupon	Coupon
Discount coupon	Bon de réduction
Deposit	Dépôt
Installment	Versement

Interest-free installment	Versement sans intérêt
Exchange	Échange
Quality	Qualité
Quantity	Quantité
Variety	Variété
Unbox	Déballage
Exchange rate	Taux de change
Local currency	Monnaie locale
Dollars	Dollars
Euros	Euros
Wholesale discount	Remise de gros
Unit discount	Remise à l'unité
Shop owner	Propriétaire du magasin
Credit card points	Points de carte de crédit
Credit card miles	Miles de carte de crédit
Loyalty points	Points de fidélité
Return	Retour
Return policy	Politique de retour
Defect	Défaut
Sleeve	Manches
Long sleeve	Manche longue
Short sleeve	Manches courtes
Sleeveless	Sans manche
Shopping kart	Chariot de supermarché
ATM	GAB
Watch	Montre
Wristwatch	Montre-bracelet
Bracelet	Bracelet
Shoe	Chaussure
Sole	Semelle
Shoelace	Lacet
High heel	Talon haut
Sandal / Flip flops	Sandales / Tongs
Ring	Bague
Earrings	Boucles d'oreilles
Hat	Chapeau
Beach hat	Chapeau de plage

Bag	Sac à main
Scarf	Echarpe
Sweater	Chandail
Coat	Manteau
Wallet	Portefeuille
Purse	Porte-monnaie
Shirt	Chemise
T-shirt	T-shirt
Skirt	Jupe
Dress	Robe
Pants	Pantalon
Suit	Costume
Belt	Ceinture
Formal shoes	Chaussures de ville
Sneakers	Baskets
Swimsuit	Maillot de bain
Lingerie	Lingerie
Underwear	Sous-vêtements
Baseball cap	Casquette de baseball
Headphones	Casque d'écoute
Speaker	Haut-parleur
Phone	Téléphone
Computer	Ordinateur
Laptop	Ordinateur portable
Book	Livre
Bestseller book	Livre le plus vendu
Inventory	Inventaire
Customer satisfaction	Satisfaction du client
Review	Revue de presse
Product review	Revue de produit
Store review	Revue du magasin
Order number	Numéro de commande
Date of delivery	Date de livraison
Receipt verification	Vérification du reçu
Cashier	Caissier
Free sale	Vente libre
Value for money	Rapport qualité-prix

Seasonal sale	Vente saisonnière
Brand logo	Logo de la marque
Price comparison	Comparaison des prix
Fitting room	Salle d'essayage
Manager	Gérant
Sale advisor	Conseiller de vente
Consumer protection	Protection des consommateurs
Price adjustment	Ajustement des prix
Free trial	Essai gratuit
Offer	Offre
On sale	En vente
Advertisement	Publicité
Reward program	Programme de récompense
Order confirmation	Confirmation de commande
Withdrawal	Retrait
Money withdrawal	Retrait d'argent
Window-shop	Vitrine de magasin

Chapter 8
Drugstores and Hospital Visits in French-Speaking Countries

While French-speaking countries are known for their rich culinary traditions, stunning landscapes, and vibrant culture, it's important to be prepared for unexpected situations such as medical emergencies. Whether you find yourself in need of medication at a local drugstore or seeking assistance in a hospital, navigating the healthcare system in a foreign country can be overwhelming, especially when faced with language barriers.

In this chapter, we will provide you with essential phrases and vocabulary to help you communicate effectively in French when visiting drugstores or seeking medical assistance. From expressing your symptoms and concerns to understanding medication instructions and discussing treatments with healthcare professionals, this guide aims to equip you with the necessary language skills to ensure a positive experience during medical visits in French-speaking countries.

While we hope that you never have to use these phrases for yourself, we recognize that unforeseen circumstances can arise during your travels. Whether it's a sudden illness, a minor injury, or any other unexpected situation, knowing how to communicate your needs and understand medical information in French can make all the difference in receiving the care you need. So, rest assured that with the help of this chapter, you'll be prepared for any medical situation that may come your way during your time in France or any other French-speaking destination.

Common Phrases	Translation
I need help.	J'ai besoin d'aide.
I need medical help.	J'ai besoin d'une aide médicale.
I need to see a doctor.	J'ai besoin de voir un médecin.
I need to go to a hospital.	Je dois aller à l'hôpital.
Please, call a doctor.	S'il vous plaît, appelez un médecin.
Please, take me to an emergency room.	S'il vous plaît, emmenez-moi aux urgences.
I have so much pain.	J'ai très mal.
I have fever.	J'ai de la fièvre.
I have a headache.	J'ai mal à la tête.
I have a back pain.	J'ai mal au dos.
My feet hurt.	J'ai mal aux pieds.
I have a stomachache.	J'ai mal à l'estomac.
My belly hurts.	J'ai mal au ventre.
I have cramps.	J'ai des crampes.
I broke my arm.	Je me suis cassé le bras.
I broke my shoulder.	Je me suis cassé l'épaule.
I broke my leg.	Je me suis cassé la jambe.
I need to vomit.	J'ai envie de vomir.
I have nauseas.	J'ai des nausées.
I feel dizzy.	J'ai le vertige.

I am going to throw up.	Je vais vomir.
I have diarrhea.	J'ai la diarrhée.
I am dehydrated.	Je suis déshydraté(e).
I have a running nose.	J'ai le nez qui coule. / Mon nez coule.
I have an allergy.	J'ai une allergie.
I have a cold.	J'ai un rhume.
I'm in too much pain to move.	J'ai trop mal pour bouger.
I have diabetes.	Je suis diabétique.
My sugar level is high.	Mon taux de sucre est élevé.
My sugar level is low.	Mon taux de sucre est bas.
My blood pressure is high.	Ma tension artérielle est élevée.
My blood pressure is low.	Ma tension artérielle est basse.
I feel weak.	Je me sens faible.
I am sick.	Je suis malade.
I am bleeding.	Je saigne.
I need a thermometer.	J'ai besoin d'un thermomètre.
Can you give me a prescription?	Pouvez-vous me donner une ordonnance ?
I need medication for…	J'ai besoin de médicaments pour…
What is the recommended dose?	Quelle est la dose recommandée ?
You need to take this pill after eating.	Vous devez prendre cette pilule après avoir mangé.
You need to take this pill before eating.	Vous devez prendre cette pilule avant de manger.
You need to take this test before having breakfast.	Vous devez faire ce test avant de prendre votre petit-déjeuner.
You need to take this test after having breakfast.	Vous devez faire ce test après le petit déjeuner.
I am allergic to…	Je suis allergique à…
I have allergies to…	J'ai des allergies à…
I need a pill to sleep.	J'ai besoin d'une pilule pour dormir.
Where can I buy this medication?	Où puis-je acheter ce médicament ?
I have a horrible hangover.	J'ai une horrible gueule de bois.
I need to drink electrolytes.	J'ai besoin de boire des électrolytes.
I need a glass of water.	J'ai besoin d'un verre d'eau.
I need dan energy drink.	J'ai besoin d'une boisson énergisante.
The patient needs to rest.	Le patient doit se reposer.
You need to rest.	Vous devez vous reposer.
I need to sleep.	J'ai besoin de dormir.
I feel weak. I need to sit.	Je me sens faible. J'ai besoin de m'asseoir.

What is the treatment?	Quel est le traitement?
What is the treatment price?	Quel est le prix du traitement ?
How long should I take the treatment?	Combien de temps dois-je prendre le traitement ?
What is the recovery period?	Quelle est la durée de récupération/ convalescence ?
The recovery is fast.	La récupération/ convalescence est rapide.
The recovery is generally slow.	La récupération /convalescence est généralement lente.
Do I need to register as a patient?	Dois-je m'inscrire en tant que patient ?
Where is the hospital?	Où se trouve l'hôpital ?
Where is the clinic?	Où se trouve la clinique ?
Where is the drugstore?	Où se trouve la pharmacie ?
You need to wait for the doctor.	Vous devez attendre le médecin.
The nurse Will take your information.	L'infirmière prendra vos coordonnées.
I need to be hospitalized.	Je dois être hospitalisé(e).
This is my information.	Voici mes informations.
These are my documents.	Voici mes documents.
The information of my medical insurance is here.	Les informations relatives à mon assurance médicale sont ici.
I don't have a medical insurance.	Je n'ai pas d'assurance médicale.
I have a medical insurance.	J'ai une assurance médicale.
I need a blood test.	J'ai besoin d'une prise de sang/test de sang,
Can I buy this medication without a prescription?	Puis-je acheter ce médicament sans ordonnance ?
You can't do exercise for a month.	Vous ne pouvez pas faire de sport pendant un mois.
You can't eat greasy food for a month.	Vous ne pouvez pas manger de nourriture grasse pendant un mois.
You can't consume alcoholic drinks for a month.	Vous ne pouvez pas consommer de boissons alcoolisées pendant un mois.
You can't make any physical effort for a month.	Vous ne pouvez faire aucun effort physique pendant un mois.
I need to go to a dentist.	Je dois aller chez le dentiste.
It is uncomfortable.	C'est inconfortable.
It is a severe pain.	C'est une douleur intense.
I am not sick. I have a hangover.	Je ne suis pas malade. J'ai la gueule de bois.
Where can I see my medical records?	Où puis-je consulter mon dossier médical ?
When Will I get the results?	Quand aurai-je les résultats ?

What is the diagnosis?	Quel est le diagnostic ?
I have itching.	J'ai des démangeaisons.
Where can I buy a thermometer?	Où puis-je acheter un thermomètre ?
Where can I buy an oximeter?	Où puis-je acheter un oxymètre ?
I can't breathe.	Je ne peux pas respirer.
Please, call an ambulance.	S'il vous plaît, appelez une ambulance.
How do you feel?	Comment vous sentez-vous ?
I feel…	Je me sens…
How did the accident happen?	Comment l'accident est-il arrivé ?
Where did the accident happen?	Où est arrive l'accident ?
What happened after?	Que s'est-il passé après ?
Does your head hurt?	Est-ce que votre tête vous fait mal ?
Does your body hurt?	Votre corps vous fait mal ?
Do you have or have you had fever?	Avez-vous ou avez-vous eu de la fièvre ?
Can you give me an ID card?	Pouvez-vous me donner une carte d'identité ?
I sprained my ankle.	Je me suis tordu la cheville.
I need a wheelchair.	J'ai besoin d'un fauteuil roulant.
I think I broke my arm.	Je pense que je me suis cassé(e) le bras.
I broke my leg.	Je me suis cassé(e) la jambe.
I have symptoms of food poisoning.	J'ai les symptômes d'une intoxication alimentaire.
My eyes are red.	Mes yeux sont rouges.
I have a throat infection.	J'ai une infection à la gorge.
I have a urinary tract infection.	J'ai une infection des voies urinaires.
The remedy is not working.	Le remède ne fonctionne pas.
You need a surgery.	Vous devez subir une intervention chirurgicale.
You need to go back to your country.	Vous devez retourner dans votre pays.
When is your return flight?	Quand est votre vol de retour ?
In this condition, you can't fly.	Dans cet état, vous ne pouvez pas prendre l'avion.
What is your emergency contact information?	Quelles sont vos coordonnées en cas d'urgence ?
Don't worry!	Ne vous inquiétez pas !
Everything will be alright.	Tout ira bien.

Common Vocabulary	Translation
Doctor	Docteur/médecin
Nurse	Infirmier/Infirmière
Hospital	Hôpital

Clinic	Clinique
Emergency	Urgences
Emergency room	Salle d'urgences
Patient	Patient(e)
Ambulance	Ambulance
Medical test	Examen/Test médical
Test	Examen/Test
Medication	Médicament
Pill	Pilule
Syrup	Sirop
Injection	Injection
Vaccine	Vaccin
Consultation	Consultation
Hospital room	Chambre d'hôpital
Drugstore	Pharmacie
Diagnosis	Diagnostic
Painkiller	Analgésique/Anti-douleur
Rash	Éruption
Sleeping pill	Somnifère
Thermometer	Thermomètre
Blood pressure	Pression artérielle
Blood pressure monitor	Tensiomètre
Vitamin	Vitamine
Type	Type
Dose	Dose
Side effects	Effets secondaires
How to take it	Comment le prendre
After eating	Après avoir mangé
Before eating	Avant de manger
After the shower	Après la douche
Before the shower	Avant la douche
Expiration date	Date d'expiration
Warning	Avertissement
Oximeter	Oxymètre
Storage instructions	Instructions de stockage
Hangover	Gueule de bois
Hangover remedy	Remedio para la resaca/cruda

Water	Remède contre la gueule de bois
Dehydration	Déshydratation
Dehydrated	Déshydraté(e)
Pain	Douleur
Headache	Mal de tête
Body ache	Courbatures
Pain in the back	Douleur dans le dos
Pain in the neck	Douleur dans le cou
Stomachache	Maux d'estomac
Bellyache	Mal au ventre
Pain in the feet	Douleur aux pieds
Pain in the hands	Douleur aux mains
Food poisoning	Intoxication alimentaire
Vomit	Vomissement
Diarrhea	Diarrhée
Intoxication/poisoning	Intoxication/empoisonnement
Treatment	Traitement
To be in pain	Souffrir
Recovery	Récupération/convalescence
X-rays	Rayons X
Tomography	Tomographie
Medical record	Dossier médical
Anesthesia	Anesthésie
Surgery	Chirurgie
Surgeon	Chirurgien
Medical insurance	Assurance médicale
Insurance bill	Facture d'assurance
Medical staff	Personnel médical
Medical assessment	Evaluation/Bilan médical
Fracture	Fracture
Broken arm	Bras cassé
Broken leg	Jambe cassée
Wheelchair	Fauteuil roulant
Burn	Brûler
Wound	Blessure
Accident	Accident
Traffic accident	Accident de la route/Accident de la circulation

Fall	Tomber
Reaction	Réaction
Allergic reaction	Réaction allergique
Treatment reaction	Réaction au traitement
General doctor	Docteur/Médecin généraliste
Obstetrician/ Gynecologist	Gynécologue obstétricien
Dentist	Dentiste
Blood type	Groupe sanguin
Infection	Infection
Effect	Effet
Medicinal effect	Effet médicinal
COVID test	Test COVID
Pregnancy test	Test de grossesse
STD	MST
Liquid	Líquide
Doctor prescription	Prescription médicale/Ordonnance du médecin
Syringe	Seringue
Diet	Régime
Supplementary diet	Régime complémentaire
Electrolytes	Électrolytes
Adverse reaction	Effet indésirable
Medication abuse	Abus de médicaments
Alcohol addiction	Addiction à l'alcool
Symptoms	Symptômes
Hangover symptoms	Symptômes de la gueule de bois
Symptoms of intoxication	Symptômes d'intoxication
Symptoms of food poisoning	Symptômes d'intoxication alimentaire
Detox drink	Boisson détox
Dizziness	Vertiges
Nauseas	Nausées
Prevention	Prévention
Gloves	Gants
Vomit bag	Sac à vomi
Remedy	Remède
Alcohol	Alcool
Shoulder	Épaule
Ankle	Cheville

Eyes	Yeux
Sleep	Dormir
Treatment plan	Plan/Programme de traitement
Hospital bill	Facture d'hôpital
Covered by the insurance	Couvert par l'assurance
Blood	Sang
Blood tests	Analyses de sang/Tests sanguins
Patient information	Informations sur les patients
See a doctor	Voir un docteur
Consult with a doctor	Consulter un docteur

Chapter 9
vocabulary related to various aspects of everyday life

In this chapter, we will delve into different vocabulary related to various aspects of everyday life and travel experiences in French-speaking countries. From describing parts of the house to discussing animals, airports, vacations, types of transport, and tours, this chapter aims to enrich your vocabulary and enhance your understanding of the French language in diverse contexts.

By learning key terms related to these topics, you will be better equipped to navigate conversations, interact with locals, and immerse yourself in the cultural nuances of French-speaking environments. Whether you're exploring the streets of Paris, enjoying a vacation in the French Riviera, or embarking on a tour of historical landmarks, having a solid grasp of this vocabulary will enhance your overall experience and enable you to communicate more effectively with French speakers.

With a focus on practical language skills, this chapter is designed to equip you with the tools necessary to confidently engage with different aspects of daily life, travel, and cultural activities in French-speaking countries. So, let's dive in and expand your linguistic repertoire to fully embrace the richness of the French language and its diverse applications in various settings.

Vocabulary related to parts of the house

maison	house
plafond	ceiling
toit	roof
cuisine	kitchen
chambre à coucher	bedroom
salon	living room
salle à manger	dining room
salle de bain	bathroom
hall	hall
escaliers	stairs
jardín	garden
garage	garage
fenêtre	window
rideau	curtain
porte	door
tapis	carpet
lampe	lamp
table	table
chaise	chair

Kitchen appliances / cookware:

cuisinière	stove
réfrigérateur	refrigerator
lave-vaisselle	dishwasher
plat	plate
verre/tasse	glass / cup
couverts en argent	silverware
fourchette	fork
couteau	knife
cuillère	spoon

tasse	cup
carafe	jug
serviettes de table	napkins
nappe	tablecloth
pot	pot
ouvre-boîte	can opener
cafetière	coffee maker
micro-ondes	microwave oven
four	oven
armoires	cabinets
vase	vase

Vocabulary related to animals

araignée	spider
aigle	eagle
cochon	pig
Poule	chicken
mouton	sheep
cheval	horse
chat	cat
Chien	dog
éléphant	elephant

lion	lion
lapin	rabbit
Souris/rat	mouse
zèbre	zebra
éléphant	elephant
girafe	giraffe
hipoppotame	hipoppotamus
chameau	camel
oiseaux	birds
serpents	snakes
poissons	fish
tortue	tortoise
lion	lion
tigre	tigre

In most cases, sentences expressing surprise or related to amazement at the appearance and size of the animals are used. In French, they are:

Regardez ! Quelle grande girafe !	Look! What a big giraffe!
Wow, quels beaux oiseaux !	Wow!, how beautiful birds!
Ces serpents me font peur !	Those snakes scare me!
Fais attention, ne t'approche pas du lac !	Be careful, don't go near the lake!
Est-ce que je peux prendre une photo des animaux ?	Can I take a photo of the animals?

Vocabulary related to airports

comptoir de la compagnie aérienne	airline counter
avion	plane
passeport	passport
carte d'embarquement	boarding pass
billet	ticket
valises	suitcases
passager	passenger
voyageur	traveler
compagnie aérienne	airline

aéroport	airport
porte d'embarquement	boarding gate

There are also expressions like:

Puis-je voir votre passeport ?	Can I see your passport?
Oui, le voici	Yes, is here
Combien de voyageurs sont présents ?	How many people are traveling?
Où voyagez-vous ?	Where are you traveling?
Votre porte d'embarquement est le numéro (xx)	Your boarding gate is number (xx)
Vous pouvez déposer vos bagages ici	You can put your luggage here
Voici les étiquettes pour les bagages	Here are the luggage tags

Vocabulary related to vacations

When learning French for English speakers, it is important to consider the variations in seasons across French-speaking countries. While some countries have distinct four seasons like in English-speaking countries, others may have only two seasons. This difference can influence the vocabulary and the way travelers describe their experiences.

Understanding the vocabulary related to holidays and seasons in French is essential for English speakers visiting France and other French-speaking countries. It is important to learn words for different seasons such as spring (le printemps), summer (l'été), fall (l'automne), and winter (l'hiver) in order to effectively communicate about travel plans and experiences.

In addition to seasonal vocabulary, travelers should familiarize themselves with terms related to transportation in French-speaking regions. This includes words for ferries, planes, buses, cars, cruises, and trains. Knowing how to navigate different modes of transportation in French will be helpful for English speakers exploring France and interacting with locals.

By acknowledging these cultural and linguistic differences, English speakers can enhance their language skills and better adapt to the French-speaking world, making their travel experiences more enjoyable and fulfilling.

Vocabulary related to types of transport

bus	bus
avion	plane

train	train
ferry	ferry
bateau	ship
croisière	cruise
hélicoptère	helicopter
moto	moto

In relation to the stations where each type of transport is taken (other than airports, they are observed)

station de bus	bus station
Garede train/gare ferroviaire	train station
port de ferry	ferry port
port maritime (ou simplement port de mer)	ship port (or just sea port)
port aérien (hélicoptères)	air port (helicopters)

Observe expressions related to bus station:

Le prochain départ vers cette destination est à (time)	The next departure to this destination is at (time)
Excusez-moi, combien coûte le billet pour (destination) ? Ça coûte (xxx)	Excuse me, how much does the ticket cost to (destination)? It costs (xxx)
Transportez-vous des bagages ?	Do you carry luggage?
¿Viajan menores de edad con usted?	Des mineurs voyagent avec vous ?

Observe the type of conversation with train stations.

Où est l'entrée de la gare ?	Where is the entrance to the train station?
La gare est à deux rues de là	The train station is two blocks away
À quelle heure part le prochain train ?	What time does the next train leave?

Notice the kind of talk about seaports.

a)	Où puis-je acheter des billets pour (destination) ?	a)	Where can I purchase tickets to (destination) ?
b)	Vous pouvez les acheter dans ce kiosque	b)	You can purchase them in that box
c)	Merci beaucoup !	c)	Thank you very much!

Regarding helicopter ports, they normally offer rides, not long trips.

Vocabulary related to tours

When talking about tours, there is a large amount of vocabulary, depending on the tourist destination to which the traveler is going. Among them; beach, mountain, sports, history tours, among others, stand out.

Observe the vocabulary related to beach tours:

agence de voyage	travel agency
agent de voyage	travel agent
réservation	reservation
nombre de voyageurs	number of travelers
hôtel	hotel
cabines	cabins
plage	playa
disponibilité	availability
aller simple	one way only
aller-retour	round trip
forfaits touristiques	tourist packages

Observe a conversation related to this type of tours.

Dans l'agence de voyage...	In the travel agency...
a) Bonjour / Bonsoir, comment pouvons-nous vous aider ?	a) Good morning / good afternoon, how can we help you?
b) Bonjour ! J'aimerais connaître les destinations de plage.	b) Hello! Good morning. I would like to know the beach destinations.
c) Oh, oui, bien sûr ! Où aimeriez-vous voyager ?	c) Oh, yeah, sure! where would you like to travel?
d) Je voudrais connaître les destinations de plage en Amérique du Sud.	d) I would like to know the beach destinations in South America
e) Bien sûr ! Passez me voir, s'il vous plaît ! Votre voyage sera-t-il un aller-retour ou un aller simple ?	e) Of course! stop by, please! Will your trip be round trip, or just one way?
f) Non, un aller-retour.	f) No, round trip.
a) Bien sûr ! Nous proposons différents forfaits touristiques de ce type.	a) Sure! We offer different tourist packages of this type.
b) Merci !	b) Thank you!

French Short Stories For

Language Learners

Learn and Improve Your French Comprehension and Vocabulary Through 20 Short Stories Based Off Captivating French History

Worldwide Nomad

LE GARDIEN QUI A SOUFFERT DE LA TROMPERIE

LE GARDIEN QUI A SOUFFERT DE LA TROMPERIE

À l'époque du Saint Empire romain germanique, les Francs germaniques ont commencé à réunir la majeure partie de la Gaule, qui était auparavant sous la domination romaine. Kuni était l'un des habitants de la Gaule. Il était un humble gardien de la caserne de la garnison romaine de sa ville. Les jours où il ne travaillait pas comme gardien, il s'occupait de la petite ferme qu'il possédait à la périphérie de la ville. Un jour, alors qu'il se rendait à la ferme, il rencontra un petit garçon qui gisait par terre, blessé. Il le soigna et le ramena chez lui. Le garçon s'appelait Mimi et raconta à Kuni comment il avait perdu ses parents lors d'un raid franc. Ils vécurent ensemble pendant des mois et Kuni le traita comme un fils. Une nuit, un bruit alerta les habitants de la ville de l'attaque de la garnison par des membres d'une tribu appelée les Francs, dirigée par le roi franc Clovis I. Ils battirent tous les soldats romains et les chassèrent. Kuni fut surpris de voir Mimi chevaucher avec l'armée du roi Clovis. Il comprit qu'il avait été trompé et que Mimi n'était qu'une espionne qui voulait la clé de la caserne. Dépité, il prit ses affaires et quitta la ville.

THE GATEKEEPER WHO SUFFERED DECEIT

In the time of the Holy Roman Empire, the Germanic Franks started to unite most of Gaul which was formerly under roman rule. Kuni was one of the people who lived in Gaul. He was a lowly gatekeeper at the barracks of the Roman garrison in his town. On the days when he was off his duty as a gatekeeper, he tended to a little farm that he had on the outskirts of the town. One day, on his way to the farm, he came across a little boy who lay on the floor, wounded. He treated the wounds and took the boy home. The boy's name was Mimi and he told Kuni the story of how he lost his parents in a Frankish raid. They lived together for months and Kuni treated him as a son. One night, a noise alerted the people in the town to an attack on the garrison by members of a tribe called the Franks, led by the Frankish king Clovis I. They beat up all the roman soldiers and chased them away. Kuni was surprised to see Mimi riding with King Clovis's army. He realized he had been deceived and Mimi was only a spy who wanted the key to the barracks. Dejected, he took his things and left the town.

Vocabulary

S'unir - Unite
Ferme - Farm
Anciennement - Formerly
Ville - Town
Bas - Lowly
Caserne - Barracks
Nom - Name
Fils - Son
Tendu - Tended
Clé - Key
Petit - Little
Plancher - Floor
Loin - Away
Parents - Parents

COMPREHENSION QUESTIONS

Quelle était la profession de Kuni? What was Kuni's occupation?

Pourquoi Kuni a-t-il ramené le garçon chez lui? Why did Kuni take the boy home?

Quelle était la véritable identité de Mimi? What was Mimi's real identity?

HISTORICAL NOTES

The Germanic Franks were a barbarian tribe who raided Gaul, a territory under the Roman Empire. The Frankish King Clovis I united most of Gaul in the late 5th century and enabled Frankish rule and dominance in the territory for centuries.

LA MONNAIE DE LA SAGESSE

Lorsque Charlemagne est devenu roi des Francs, les domaines francs étaient très divisés. Chaque faction voulait prendre le contrôle et Charlemagne a dû mener des guerres avec les Lombards, la Bavière et d'autres. Ses ennemis sont très nombreux et son armée est affaiblie par tant de guerres. Pourtant, les guerres se sont poursuivies pendant des années et ne semblaient pas avoir de fin. Les ennemis de Charlemagne étaient également fatigués et ils l'ont tous invité à une réunion. Lors de cette réunion, ils discutent d'un moyen de mettre fin à la guerre et de désigner un vainqueur. Après de longues discussions, ils décidèrent de mettre en place une épreuve. Celui qui parviendrait à faire reconnaître le pape comme roi gagnerait la guerre. Le pape était un vieil homme têtu qui n'appréciait aucun des chefs de guerre. Les autres sont allés voir le pape avec des cadeaux en or, en argent, en épices et en fruits exotiques. Charlemagne savait que le pape ne serait pas touché par les choses matérielles. Il lui rendait donc visite tous les soirs et ils s'asseyaient ensemble pour discuter de théologie et de philosophie. Émerveillé par la sagesse et l'humilité de Charlemagne, le pape le nomme roi des Francs.

THE WISDOM CURRENCY

When Charlemagne became King of the Franks, there was a lot of division in the Frankish domains. Each faction wanted to take control and Charlemagne had to fight wars with Lombards, Bavaria, and some others. His enemies were very many and his army was weakened from fighting so many wars. Yet, the wars waged on for years and there seemed to be no end. Charlemagne's enemies were also tired so they all invited him to a meeting. At the meeting they discussed a way to end the war and determine a winner. After much argument, they decided to set a test. Whoever could get the Pope to recognize him as the King would win the war. The Pope was a stubborn old man who did not care for any of the war leaders. The others went to the Pope with gifts of gold, silver, spices, and exotic fruits. Charlemagne knew the Pope would not be moved by material things so he visited him every evening and they sat together, discussing theology and philosophy. Amazed by Charlemagne's wisdom and humility, the Pope named him King of the Franks.

Vocabulary

Roi - King
Ennemi - Enemy
L'or - Gold
Division - Division
Homme - Man
Domaines - Domains
Années - Years
Argument - Argument
Fin - End
Domaines - Domains
Anciens - Old
Faction - Faction
Nombreux - Many
Têtu - Stubborn

COMPREHENSION QUESTIONS

Comment Charlemagne a-t-il impressionné le pape? How did Charlemagne impress the Pope?

Quels cadeaux les autres ont-ils apportés au pape? What gifts did others bring to the Pope?

Pourquoi les soldats étaient-ils fatigués ? Why were the soldiers tired?

HISTORICAL NOTE

Pepin the short, father of Charlemagne, established the Carolingian dynasty as the Kings of Frank. But the dynasty grew to full strength under his son. Charlemagne was King of the Franks from 768 and set up the Carolingian Empire. It was from the western part of this empire that the Medieval Kingdom of France emerged, known as West Francia.

LE CÉLÈBRE PRINCE

À l'époque où la maison Capet régnait sur le royaume de France, Philippe IV n'avait pas de fils et craignait de perdre la dynastie royale que ses prédécesseurs avaient construite et maintenue au fil des ans. Lorsque sa femme, Jeanne Ire de Navarre, donna naissance à leur dernière fille, ils gardèrent le secret sur le fait qu'il s'agissait d'une fille. Ils l'ont habillée en homme et l'ont présentée comme le prince héritier. Le peuple et les conseillers du roi se réjouissent car la naissance d'un roi est synonyme de stabilité. Le prince héritier, Philippe V, était très aimé et il a su gagner l'affection des roturiers et des nobles. Elle était habile, forte, brillante et courageuse. Cependant, tout le monde n'était pas satisfait d'elle. Sa sœur aînée savait qu'elle était une femme et complotait avec les autres sœurs pour la dénoncer. Le jour où Philippe V devait être couronné roi de France, ses sœurs écrivirent à toutes les maisons nobles du royaume et révélèrent le secret de son sexe. Philippe V ne pouvait plus être roi, ce qui mit fin au règne de la maison Capet en France.

THE CELEBRATED PRINCE

In the time when House Capet ruled the Kingdom of France, Philip IV had no sons and was afraid that he would lose the Kingship dynasty that his predecessors had built and maintained over the years. When his wife, Joan I of Navarre, gave birth to their last daughter, they kept it a secret that the baby was a girl. They dressed her up in male clothing and paraded her as the Crown Prince. The people, as well as the King's advisers were happy because the birth of a King represented stability. The Crown Prince, Philip V, was well loved and grew to command the love of both commoners and nobles. She was skilled, strong, brilliant and courageous. However, not everyone was happy with her. Her eldest sister knew the secret that she was a woman and plotted with the other sisters to expose her. On the day that Philip V was to be crowned King of France, her sisters wrote to all noble houses in the Kingdom and revealed the secret of her gender. Philip V could no longer be King and so ended the reign of House Capet in France.

VOCABULARY

Temps - Time
Royaume - Kingdom
Construit - Built
Fille - Daughter
Bébé - Baby
Prédécesseur - Predecessor
Couronne - Crown
Stabilité - Stability
Secret - Secret
Conseiller - Adviser
Fort - Strong
Heureux - Happy
Sœur - Sister
Règne - Reign

COMPREHENSION QUESTIONS

Pourquoi le roi Philippe IV était-il inquiet ? Why do you think Philip V's sisters were unhappy?

Comment la dynastie des Capet s'est-elle terminée ? Why was King Philip IV worried?

Pourquoi pensez-vous que les soeurs de Philippe V étaient malheureuses ? How did the Capet dynasty end?

HISTORICAL NOTES

Philip IV of House Capet was a notable French King for his efforts that led to the eventual transformation of France from a feudal state to a centralized early modern state. He reduced the power and wealth of the nobility and clergy by assigning the government of the Kingdom to skilled civil servants. He also elevated the authority of the monarchy by restricting his vassals and their feudal privileges. He was influential in international circles for his ambitious positioning of close relatives to take foreign thrones. He had three sons who all became King of France but died without producing sons of their own. Thus, the dynasty of House Capet ended.

LE FILS DE LA PAIX

Pendant la guerre de Cent Ans, un conflit qui a duré 116 ans, de nombreuses personnes ont été enrôlées dans l'armée contre leur gré. Un garçon nommé Michée vivait en France. Apprenti cordonnier, il était apprécié des autres ouvriers et des jeunes garçons de la ville. Un jour, un général de l'armée est venu dans la ville et a appelé les noms de plusieurs garçons, dont celui de Michée, qui ont été forcés de s'engager dans l'armée. Pendant la guerre, de nombreux amis de Micah ont été blessés et renvoyés de l'armée. D'autres sont morts. Mais Micah s'est battu, a reçu de nombreuses récompenses et est arrivé au sommet de l'armée. Une fois que cela s'est produit, Michée a réuni tous les soldats sous ses ordres et leur a dit qu'ils ne participeraient plus à la guerre. Il considérait que la guerre était une perte de temps et qu'elle servait les intérêts de nobles qui ne voulaient même pas se battre. Il s'entretient avec le chef de l'armée anglaise, avec lequel il s'était lié d'amitié, et les soldats anglais refusent également de se battre. Les dirigeants français et anglais sont contraints de tenir une réunion diplomatique et de régler leurs problèmes sans autre forme de conflit armé. Michée fut célébré dans les deux nations comme le héros qui avait mis fin à la guerre et nommé le Fils de la Paix.

THE SON OF PEACE

During the Hundred Years' War, a conflict that lasted 116 years, many people were conscripted into the army against their will. There was a boy named Micah who lived in France. He was a shoemaker's apprentice who was popular among the other workers and young boys in the town. One day, an army general came to the town and called out the names of several boys, Micah included, who were forced to join the army. At war, many of Micah's friends were injured and sent away from the army. Others died. But Micah fought on, receiving many awards and getting to the top position in the army. Once this happened, Micah called together all the soldiers under him and told them that they would no longer be fighting in the war. He saw the war as a waste of their time and for the profit of nobles who would not even engage in fighting. He spoke with the leader of the English army, whom he had befriended and the English soldiers also refused to fight. The French and English leaders were forced to hold a diplomatic meeting and settle their problems without further armed conflict. Micah was celebrated in both nations as the hero who ended the war and named the Son of Peace.

VOCABULARY

Déchets - Waste
Populaire - Popular
En route - Away
Problème - Problem
Plus loin - Further
Profit - Profit
Contre - Against
Régler - Settle
Conflit - Conflict
Héros - Hero
Diplomatique - Diplomatic
Nation - Nation
Plusieurs - Several
Général - General

COMPREHENSION QUESTIONS

Comment Micah a-t-il terminé la guerre ? How did Micah end the war?

Qu'est-il arrivé aux amis de Michée pendant la guerre ? What happened to Micah's friends during the war?

Quelle était la raison de la guerre ? What was the reason for the war?

HISTORICAL NOTE

The Hundred Years' War spanned the years 1337-1453. It was a series of armed conflict between England and France. It was a war of succession that resulted from English claims to the French Throne and the lack of a heir to succeed the Capet Dynasty. Although it lasted for 116 years, there were several years of truces between the conflicts.

LE ROI CUPIDE

Le roi Louis est connu dans toute la France comme un souverain méchant. Il s'assurait d'être la personne la plus puissante du pays et emprisonnait tous ceux qui tentaient de s'opposer à lui. Il n'écoutait jamais ses conseillers et menait des politiques dures qui laissaient le peuple souffrir tandis que lui et ses amis s'enrichissaient. Un jardinier travaillait pour le roi. Il s'appelait Henri et servait avec diligence, même s'il était peu payé. Il avait besoin d'argent pour s'occuper de sa fille unique, Maria, et l'envoyer à l'école. Un jour, comme Henri était malade mais que le roi ne le laissait pas travailler, Maria lui apporta secrètement des médicaments et de la nourriture. Cependant, le roi aperçut Maria et ordonna à ses gardes de l'arrêter et de l'emmener dans ses appartements. Il était tombé amoureux d'elle et voulait la prendre pour épouse, mais Maria l'a refusé. Elle ne voulait pas épouser un homme qui volait son peuple et le faisait souffrir. Furieux, le roi Louis menaça de la faire tuer. Lorsque Henri entendit cela, il prit peur et demanda de l'aide à ses amis. Ceux-ci rassemblèrent tous les habitants de la ville et du palais. Ils renvoyèrent le roi et nommèrent à sa place un souverain juste et équitable.

THE GREEDY KING

King Louis was known in all of France as a wicked ruler. He made sure he was the single most powerful person in the country and imprisoned all those who tried to oppose him. He never listened to his advisors and made harsh policies that let the people suffer while he and his friends grew rich. There was a gardener who worked for the King. His name was Henry and he served diligently, although he was paid little. He needed the money to take care of his only daughter, Maria, and send her to school. One day, because Henry was sick but the King would not let him off work, Maria brought him medicine and food secretly. However, the King happened to see Maria and he ordered his guards to arrest her and take her into his rooms. He had fallen in love with her and wanted to take her as his wife but Maria refused him. She would not marry a man who stole from his people and made them suffer. Angered, King Louis threatened to have her killed. When Henry heard of this, he became afraid and asked his friends for help. They gathered all the people of the city and to the palace. They sent the King away and appointed a fair and just ruler in his place.

VOCABULARY

Connu - Known
Peur - Afraid
Amour - Love
Méchant - Wicked
Épouser - Marry
Célibataire - Single
Palais - Palace
École - School
Puissant - Powerful
Peuple - People
Gardes - Guards
Pays - Country
Dure - Harsh
Politique - Policy

COMPREHENSION QUESTIONS

Pourquoi Henri travaillait-il au palais ? Why did Henry work at the palace?

Pourquoi Maria rendait-elle visite à son père au travail ? Why did Maria visit her father at work?

Qu'est-il arrivé au roi Louis ? What happened to King Louis?

HISTORICAL NOTE

The absolute centralized monarchy in France lasted from the late 15th century to the late 18th century. It was marked by a strong, centralized authority which was vested in the monarchs. The kings exercised absolute power and control over the government, economy and society.

LE CHOC DES RELIGIONS

Le roi François Ier était un homme juste et sage qui se souciait beaucoup du bien-être de son pays et de son peuple. Il a toujours fait de son mieux pour maintenir la paix et la stabilité et le peuple aimait son règne. Mais cela n'a pas duré longtemps. Une nouvelle religion a été introduite parmi le peuple et elle semblait aller à l'encontre de la religion populaire dans le pays. Auparavant, le catholicisme était la seule religion légalement reconnue, mais peu à peu, le peuple a commencé à se convertir au christianisme protestant. Certains citoyens et membres de la noblesse ont fait part au roi de leurs plaintes concernant la foi protestante. Ils demandaient que tous ceux qui acceptaient cette religion soient emprisonnés. Mais le roi a fait preuve de sagesse en déclarant que les protestants avaient le droit d'avoir leurs croyances, tant qu'elles ne menaçaient pas ou ne nuisaient pas aux autres religions. La paix règne pendant un certain temps, jusqu'au jour où les protestants placardent des tracts dans tout le pays. Dans ces tracts, ils condamnent les croyances catholiques. Furieux, les catholiques ont pris les armes et ont commencé à attaquer les protestants autour d'eux. Cela a conduit à une guerre généralisée et a mis en échec les efforts du roi pour maintenir la paix.

THE CLASH OF RELIGIONS

King Francis I was a just and wise man who cared greatly for the welfare of his country and his people. He always did his best to maintain peace and stability and the people loved his rule. However, this was not to last long. A new religion was introduced among the people and it seemed to go against the popular religion in the country. Formerly, Catholicism was the only lawfully recognized religion, but slowly the people began to convert to Protestant Christianity. Some citizens and members of the nobility brought their complaints about the Protestant faith to the king. They demanded that everybody who accepted this religion should be imprisoned. But the king showed his wisdom by declaring that the Protestants are allowed to have their beliefs, as long as they do not threaten or harm other religions. Peace reigned for a while until one day, the Protestants posted flyers all over the country. In the flyers, they condemned catholic beliefs. Angry, the Catholics picked up arms and began to attack Protestants around them. This led to a blown out war and defeated the king's efforts to maintain peace.

VOCABULARY

Sagesse - Wisdom
Bien-être - Welfare
Croyance - Belief
Noblesse - Nobility
Le mal - Harm
La religion - Religion
Juste - Just
Stabilité - Stability
Attaquer - Attack
Menacer - Threaten
En colère - Angry
Maintenir - Maintain
Effort - Effort
Vaincu - Defeated

COMPREHENSION QUESTIONS

Comment le roi François a-t-il empêché les conflits entre catholiques et protestants ? How did King Francis prevent conflict between the Catholics and the Protestants?

Quelle était la religion légalement reconnue dans le pays ? What was the lawfully recognized religion in the country?

Le roi François a-t-il réussi à empêcher la guerre ? Did King Francis succeed in preventing war?

HISTORICAL NOTES

The French Wars of Religion is the name given to a period of conflicts between the Catholics and the Protestants. Protestant ideas were first introduced during the reign of King Francis I and although he was firmly opposed to them, he did his best to maintain a middle ground in order to prevent the situation from escalating into conflict. However, as the Huguenot Protestants gained more ground, the Catholic hostility increased against them. Eventually it escalated into conflict and resulted in eight civil wars with periods of peace in between.

LA CONVOITISE DU TRÔNE

Le roi Henri II de France a eu cinq fils. Son quatrième fils, Henri III, était exclu des affaires du pays car il avait trois frères aînés et personne ne pensait qu'il deviendrait un jour roi de France. Bien qu'il ne soit pas le plus intelligent, le plus fort ou le plus courageux des princes, il fait preuve d'une douceur qui incite les gens à lui faire confiance et à le respecter. C'est pourquoi il a été élu monarque du Commonwealth polono-lituanien. Il y mena une vie de souverain agréable, jouissant de la richesse et de l'autorité. À la mort de son dernier frère aîné, Charles, qui régnait sur la France, tout le monde s'attendait à ce qu'il laisse son jeune frère monter sur le trône. Il les surprend en abandonnant la Pologne-Lituanie et devient roi de France. Malheureusement, cela se passe pendant les conflits entre les catholiques et les protestants. Lorsque le dernier frère d'Henri, François, meurt et qu'Henri ne peut pas produire d'héritier, une guerre de succession éclate. Les catholiques refusent de laisser le cousin d'Henri, qui est protestant, monter sur le trône. La guerre a conduit à la mort d'Henri et son cousin, Henri IV, est monté sur le trône après s'être converti au catholicisme.

COVETING THE THRONE

King Henry II of France had five sons. His fourth son, Henry III, was excluded from the affairs of the country as he had three older brothers and nobody thought he would ever become king of France. Although he was not the smartest, strongest or bravest of the princes, he exhibited a gentle demeanor that made people trust and respect him. Because of this, he was elected as monarch of the Polish-Lithuanian commonwealth. There he had a good life as a ruler and enjoyed wealth and authority. On the death of his last elder brother, Charles, who had been ruling France, everyone expected that he would let his younger brother take the throne. He surprised them by abandoning Poland-Lithuania and became the King of France. Unfortunately, this was during the conflicts between the Catholics and the Protestants. When Henry's last remaining brother, Francis, died and Henry could not produce an heir, a war of succession broke out. The Catholics refused to let Henry's cousin who was a protestant take over the throne. The war led to Henry's eventual death and his cousin, Henry IV, assumed the throne after converting to Catholicism.

VOCABULARY

Exclus - Excluded
Affaire - Affair
Plus ancien - Older
Personne - Nobody
Doux - Gentle
Princes - Princes
Mort - Death
Le plus courageux - Bravest
Frère - Brother
Comportement - Demeanor
Trône - Throne
Autorité - Authority
Héritier - Heir
Succession - Succession

COMPREHENSION QUESTIONS

Pourquoi les gens ont-ils été surpris qu'Henri abandonne son poste d'élu ? Why did it surprise people that Henry abandoned his elected post?

Qu'est-ce qui a conduit à la mort d'Henri ? What led to Henry's death?

Qu'est-ce qui a conduit à la mort d'Henri ? How did Henry's brother end up becoming the King?

HISTORICAL NOTE

During the Wars of Religion, a succession crisis broke out in France. It involved Henry III, the last of the Valois line, fighting against factions of the House of Bourbon and the House of Guise. It resulted in the eventual death of Henry II and Henry III, his cousin and the Bourbon King of Navarre, won the conflict.

CONTES DE LAYE LE VOYAGEUR

Il était une fois un garçon qui s'appelait Laye. Il vivait au XIXe siècle, à l'époque où la France avait commencé à étendre ses tentacules sur le monde et à prendre d'autres territoires comme colonies. Toute sa vie, Laye a voulu explorer le monde qui l'entourait. Petit garçon, il ne pouvait jamais rester en place, toujours désireux de savoir ce qui se trouvait au-delà de la prochaine colline et quels secrets la forêt cachait. À dix-huit ans, il s'est engagé dans l'armée coloniale pour faire partie des troupes qui se rendraient dans les pays étrangers et apporteraient la civilisation à leurs habitants. Avec sa compagnie, il se rend d'abord à Hanoï, dont il explore les rues tout en accomplissant sa mission. Il y rencontre Liem, un jeune vietnamien, qui lui fait visiter la ville et avec qui il se lie d'amitié. Il est triste de se séparer de son cher ami lorsque sa compagnie est transférée, mais il va de l'avant, impatient d'explorer de nouvelles contrées. Sa compagnie s'est ensuite rendue en Afrique, où il s'est fortement imprégné de la culture, de la vitalité de ses habitants et de la beauté de ses terres. Cependant, il ne peut ignorer les actes de cruauté, tels que la traite des esclaves et le travail forcé, perpétrés par l'empire français à la recherche de richesses. Il se rend compte de l'impact du processus colonial sur la vie des habitants de ces terres et se promet de faire quelque chose pour changer cela. Au fur et à mesure qu'il prenait du grade, Laye s'est engagé à mettre en œuvre des politiques moins cruelles et est devenu par la suite une voix active contre le colonialisme.

TALES OF LAYE THE TRAVELER

There was once a boy named Laye. He lived in the 19th century, at the time when France had started to spread its tentacles over the world and take other territories as it colonies. All his life Laye wanted to explore the world around him. As a little boy he could never sit still, always eager to know what lay beyond the next hill and what secrets the forest hid. When he became eighteen, he signed up to join the colonial army as part of the expenditure that would travel to foreign lands and bring civilization to its people. First, he and his company visited Hanoi, exploring the streets of Hanoi as they went about their duties. There, he met Liem, a young Vietnamese local, who showed him around the place and they became as close as brothers. He was sad to part with his dear friend when his company was transferred but he moved on, eager to explore new lands. His company visited Africa next, where he found himself greatly immersed in the culture, the vibrancy of its people and the beauty of the lands. Yet, he could not ignore the acts of cruelty such as slave trade and forced labor that were carried out by the French empire in the pursuit of wealth. He realized the impact the colonial process had on the lives of people who lived in these lands and vowed to do something to change this. As he grew in rank, Laye committed himself to implementing less cruel policies and later became an active voice that spoke against colonialism.

VOCABULARY

Ami - Friend
Rang - Rank
Politiques - Policies
Devoirs - Duty
Société - Company
Cruel - Cruel
Terre - Land
Poursuite - Pursuit
Étranger - Foreign
Répandre - Spread
Mettre en œuvre - Implement
Voixn - Voice
Colonialisme - Colonialism
Au-delà - Beyond

COMPREHENSION QUESTIONS

Pourquoi Laye s'est-il engagé dans les dépenses ? Why did Laye join the expenditures?

En quoi les voyages de Laye l'ont-ils changé ? How did Laye's travels change him?

Quelle leçon importante Laye a-t-il apprise au cours de son voyage ? What important lesson did Laye learn during his journey?

HISTORICAL NOTE

France built its colonial empire starting from the 16th century when it started to exert authority over overseas territories. It established its presence in North America, the Caribbean and India in the 17th century but could not keep its territories following defeat in the Seven Years' War.

France participated in the Berlin Conference of 1884, where it was officially awarded some African territories. Here it took advantage of the natural resources to establish itself as a powerful empire and also spread the French Language and Catholic faith through the policy of assimilation.

AMÉLIE AU GRAND CŒUR

Les temps sont durs en France. Les membres de la classe inférieure se sentent floués par la noblesse. C'est une période de difficultés économiques, mais les ouvriers en souffrent davantage, car la plupart des revenus du pays profitent aux riches. Le pays est en proie à des tensions, car les travailleurs réclament l'égalité. Amelia était une couturière qui travaillait pour une famille aristocrate. Elle confectionnait tous leurs vêtements et elle était bien payée. Elle servait également d'infirmière à deux des plus jeunes filles. La famille l'aimait beaucoup et la traitait avec respect, mais elle ne se rendait pas compte des difficultés de sa vie quotidienne. Elle luttait pour nourrir sa famille de quatre enfants et sa mère malade, et ne pouvait pas passer assez de temps avec ses enfants parce qu'elle passait le plus clair de son temps à travailler pour la famille aristocrate. Un jour, les tensions entre la classe ouvrière et l'aristocratie ont éclaté et les ouvriers ont commencé à attaquer les membres de l'aristocratie. Amelia a pris peur pour la famille aristocrate qu'elle servait et les a tous cachés chez elle, les nourrissant avec le peu qu'elle pouvait s'offrir. En vivant avec Amelia, ils réalisèrent à quel point ils étaient privilégiés et se promirent de faire mieux. Malheureusement, la nouvelle s'est répandue qu'Amelia cachait des aristocrates dans sa maison et les gens ont exigé qu'elle les dénonce. Elle a refusé et a plaidé avec les travailleurs. Elle leur a fait comprendre que la seule façon d'assurer l'égalité n'était pas de faire du mal aux aristocrates, mais de travailler ensemble.

KINDHEARTED AMELIE

It was a tough time in France. Members of the lower class felt cheated by the nobility. It was a time of economic hardship but the workers suffered it more, as most of the revenue the country made was enjoyed by the wealthy. The country was alive with tension as the workers clamored for equality. Amelia was a seamstress who worked for an aristocratic family. She made all their clothing and they paid her well. She also served as a nurse to two of the younger daughters. The family liked her greatly and treated her respectfully, yet they were oblivious to the hardships of her daily life. She struggled to feed her family of four children and her sick mother, and could not spend enough time with her children because she spent most of her time working for the aristocratic family. One day, the tensions between the working class and the aristocracy broke into open conflict and the workers began to attack members of the aristocracy. Amelia became afraid for the aristocratic family she served and hid them all in her home, feeding them with the little she could afford. Living with Amelia made them realize how privileged they were and they vowed to do better. Sadly, word got out that Amelia was hiding aristocrats in her home and people demanded that she turn them in. She refused and pleaded with the workers. She let them know that the only way to ensure equality was not to harm aristocrats but to work together.

VOCABULARY

Trompé - Cheated
Riche - Wealthy
Vivant - Alive
Famille - Family
Tension - Tension
Travailleur - Worker
Aristocrate - Aristocrat
Affecter - Afford
Égalité - Equality
Classe - Class
Noblesse - Nobility
Ouvert - Open
Assez - Enough
Peu - Little

COMPREHENSION QUESTIONS

Comment Amelia a-t-elle pu mettre fin au conflit ? How did Amelia potentially end the conflict?

Comment Amelia a-t-elle protégé la famille aristocrate ? How did Amelia protect the Aristocrat family?

Comment décririez-vous la relation d'Amelia avec la famille aristocrate ? How would you describe Amelia's relationship with the aristocratic family?

HISTORICAL NOTE

The French Revolution was a period characterized by tensions and conflicts which led to social and political changes. A financial crisis as well as struggle for political power only served to exacerbate the situation. It resulted in the eventual abolition of the French monarchy and saw the establishment of the French First Republic.

L'AMOUR AU TEMPS DES RÉVOLUTIONS

Zoya est issue d'une riche famille de commerçants. C'est l'époque de la Première République française et sa famille n'a pas encore oublié les pertes et les épreuves qu'elle a subies pendant les révolutions françaises. Ils nourrissent une grande aversion pour la classe ouvrière et évitent toute relation avec elle. Zoya était différente du reste de sa famille. C'est une artiste brillante et intellectuelle. Elle s'intéresse aux idées qui alimentent les réformes et se consacre à la lecture des grands penseurs et philosophes. Elle espérait découvrir des moyens d'effacer définitivement les inégalités dans la société. Un jour, elle a été invitée à une réunion secrète de collègues artistes et intellectuels. Elle y a rencontré des personnes partageant les mêmes idées et elles ont travaillé ensemble pour combler le fossé de l'inégalité. Au cours de ces réunions, elle a rencontré un jeune homme nommé Mark. Elle est tombée amoureuse de son esprit brillant. Ils s'aimaient beaucoup et, après un certain temps, elle l'a présenté à sa famille. Ses parents furent très mécontents et lui interdirent de le rencontrer. Elle n'en tint aucun compte et l'aima encore plus. Peu après, ils se marièrent et sa famille n'eut d'autre choix que de l'accepter.

LOVE IN THE TIME OF REVOLUTIONS

Zoya was from a wealthy family of merchants. It was the time of the French First Republic and her family had not yet forgotten the losses and hardship they went through during the French Revolutions. They nursed a great dislike for the working class and avoided all relations with them. Zoya was different from the rest of her family. She was a brilliant artist and an intellectual. She paid attention to the ideas that fueled reforms and dedicated herself to reading great thinkers and philosophers. She hoped to discover ways to permanently erase inequality in society. One day, she was invited to a secret meeting of fellow artists and intellectuals. There she met like minds and they worked together to close the gap of inequality. During their meetings, she met a young man named Mark. She fell in love with his bright mind. They loved each other greatly and after some time she introduced him to her family. Her parents were greatly displeased and forbade her from meeting with him. She paid them no heed and only loved him more. Shortly afterward they got married and her family had no choice but to accept him.

VOCABULARY

Différents - Different
Idées - Ideas
Intellectuel - Intellectual
L'esprit - Mind
Forbade - Forbade
Société - Society
Découvrir - Discover
Jeune - Young
Mécontent - Displeased
Choix - Choice
Accepter - Accept
Lumineux - Bright
Difficultés - Hardships
N'aime pas - Dislike

COMPREHENSION QUESTIONS

Quelle a été la réaction de la famille de Zoya face au choix de son partenaire ? What was Zoya's family's reaction to her choice of partner?

Pourquoi sa famille n'aimait-elle pas la classe ouvrière ? Why did her family dislike the working class?

Qu'est-ce qui a conduit Zoya aux réunions secrètes ? What led Zoya to the secret meetings?

HISTORICAL NOTE

The French Republic was established on the 21st September, 1792. It came to an end at the declaration of the First Empire under Napoleon.

LE PETIT ROYAUME DE RUTH

Ruth, mère célibataire de deux enfants, vivait dans un immeuble avec d'autres familles. Elle était connue pour son attitude décontractée et sa générosité. Elle travaillait comme enseignante dans l'école locale et utilisait ses maigres revenus pour s'occuper de sa famille. Chaque jour, après l'école, d'autres parents envoyaient leurs enfants à Ruth. Ils savaient qu'elle aimait s'occuper des enfants et qu'elle avait une façon discrète de les faire écouter. Elle leur apprenait des comptines pour leur rafraîchir la mémoire et les aidait à faire des additions simples. Elle préparait toujours des biscuits et donnait à chaque enfant deux gros biscuits et un verre de lait. Un jour, Ruth a parlé aux enfants des modèles à suivre. Elle leur a dit que les modèles étaient des personnes que les autres respectaient et admiraient. Lorsqu'elle a demandé aux enfants quels étaient leurs modèles, la plupart des garçons ont mentionné le général Napoléon. Ils voulaient être comme lui, combattre et gagner des guerres. Ruth a souri devant leur impatience. Elle leur a fait comprendre que c'était une bonne cause que de vouloir se battre pour son pays, mais leur a expliqué que tout le monde ne pouvait pas être soldat. Elle leur a expliqué la nécessité d'avoir des professionnels divers dans un pays et l'importance du travail le plus simple. Les enfants sont retournés chez leurs parents remplis de nouvelles connaissances.

RUTH'S LITTLE KINGDOM

Ruth was a single mother of two who lived in a building with other families. She was known for her easygoing attitude and her generosity. She worked as a teacher in the local school and used her meager income to care for her family. Every day after school, other parents would send their children to Ruth. They knew that she enjoyed looking after children and she had a quiet way of making them listen to her. She taught them rhymes to refresh their memories and helped them with simple sums. She always baked cookies and gave each child two large cookies and a glass of milk. One day, Ruth taught the children about role models. She told them that role models were people who other people respected and looked up to. When she asked the children who their role models were, most of the boys mentioned General Napoleon. They wanted to be like him, fighting and winning wars. Ruth smiled at their eagerness. She let them know it was a worthy cause to want to fight for one's country but explained to them that everyone could not be a soldier. She explained the need for having diverse professionals in a country and the importance of the simplest job. The children returned to their parents filled with new knowledge.

VOCABULARY

Unique - Single
Bâtiment - Building
Verre - Glass
Mère - Mother
Travail - Job
Attitude - Attitude
Lait - Milk
Revenu - Income
Lutte - Fight
Digne - Worthy
Sommes - Sums
Maigre - Meager
Modèle - Model
Cookies - Cookies

COMPREHENSION QUESTIONS

Quelle leçon Ruth a-t-elle enseignée aux enfants ? What lesson did Ruth teach the children?

Pourquoi les parents ont-ils envoyé leurs enfants à Ruth ? Why did the parents send their children to Ruth?

Comment décririez-vous Ruth ? How would you describe Ruth?

HISTORICAL NOTE

Napoleone di Buonaparte, later Napoleon Bonaparte was a French military popular who gained popularity during the French Revolution and led a number of successful battles during the Revolutionary Wars. He later organized a coup and took over the French government, establishing himself as Emperor of the French. Although he was a skilled army leader and won several territories for France, his humanitarian approach is regarded with controversy.

LA QUÊTE DU POUVOIR

Après la défaite de Napoléon, les membres de la noblesse ont commencé à revenir d'exil. Ils avaient fui le pays pour éviter d'être pris dans les conflits, mais ils voyaient maintenant l'occasion de revenir et de restaurer la monarchie. Ils pensaient que c'était la seule forme de gouvernement juste et bénéfique. Parmi eux se trouvait Alexandre, un homme riche qui faisait commerce de la soie et des épices. Bien qu'il ait été très riche avant de quitter le pays, il n'avait pas d'influence politique. Il voit dans son retour l'occasion d'acquérir un pouvoir politique. Il rencontre Louis de la Maison de Bourbon et lui promet un soutien financier pour monter sur le trône en échange du mariage de Louis XVIII avec sa fille unique, Marie. Louis accepte et reçoit d'importantes sommes d'argent de la part d'Alexandre. Le conseiller d'Alexandre, Joan, le met cependant en garde contre cette alliance. Il ne croit pas que Louis honorera sa promesse, car il sait qu'il aime une autre femme. Alexandre n'a pas écouté son conseiller et a continué à aider Louis avec son argent. Lorsque Louis monta enfin sur le trône, il prit pour épouse son amante secrète et fit emprisonner Alexandre afin qu'il ne soit jamais tenu responsable de sa promesse non tenue.

QUEST FOR POWER

After Napoleon was defeated, members of the nobility started to return from exile. They had fled the country to avoid being caught in the conflicts but now saw an opportunity to return and restore the monarchy. They believed it was the only right and beneficial form of government. Among them was Alexandre, a wealthy man who traded in silk and spices. Although he was very rich before leaving the country, he did not have political influence. He saw his return as an opportunity to gain political power. He met with Louis of the House of Bourbon and promised him financial support to mount the throne in return for Louis XVIII marrying his only daughter, Marie. Louis agreed to this and received large amounts of money from Alexandre. Alexandre's adviser, Joan, however warned him against the alliance. He did not believe Louis would honor his promise, he knew that he loved another woman. Alexandre paid no heed to his adviser and continued to help Louis with his money. When Louis finally took the throne, he took his secret lover as wife and had Alexandre imprisoned so that he would never be held accountable for his broken promise.

VOCABULARY

Exil - Exile
Promesse - Promise
Après - After
Opportunité - Opportunity
Retour - Return
Emprisonné - Imprisoned
Forme - Form
Gouvernement - Government
Pouvoir - Power
Restaurer - Restore
Amoureux - Lover
Jamais - Never
Influence - Influence
Argent - Money
Alliance - Alliance

VOCABULARY QUESTIONS

Pourquoi Alexandre n'a-t-il pas écouté son conseiller ? Why did Alexandre not listen to his adviser?

Quelle est l'entente entre Alexandre et Louis ? What was the deal between Alexandre and Louis?

Quel était l'objectif d'Alexandre ? What was Alexandre's aim?

HISTORICAL NOTE

The Bourbon Restoration refers to the return of Monarchical rule to France after the Napoleonic wars and the defeat of Napoleon. The monarchy sought to restore the qualities of the Ancien Regime, before the revolutions. They could however not reverse most of the reforms that had been made during the French Revolutions.

NAPOLÉON PATRIOTE

Louis Napoléon Bonaparte a grandi en lisant les récits des exploits de son cousin Napoléon II et les tristes récits de sa défaite. Il souhaite changer la situation sociale, politique et économique de son pays, mais il sait qu'il ne pourra y parvenir qu'en accédant au pouvoir. Il se consacre à l'étude, lisant des discours politiques et économiques et rencontrant de grands professeurs. Ses parents le trouvaient vraiment bizarre mais l'encourageaient quand même, l'aimant comme leur fils unique. En grandissant, il devient populaire pour ses théories politiques et, en peu de temps, il devient une voix politique de premier plan. Il devient l'empereur du Second Empire français et se met immédiatement au travail. Il met en place des politiques qui améliorent l'économie de son pays, encourageant les affaires et le sport. Il fait de la France un empire moderne et veille à l'innovation des infrastructures et des technologies. Avec le temps, la France est redevenue une autorité mondiale et tout le monde a fait l'éloge de Louis Napoléon pour les grands services qu'il a rendus en tant qu'empereur.

PATRIOTIC NAPOLEON

Louis Napoleon Bonaparte grew up reading stories of his cousin Napoleon II's exploits and the sad tales of his eventual defeat. He desired to make changes to the social, political and economic situation of his country but he knew he could only achieve this by gaining power. He devoted himself to studying, reading political and economic discourse and meeting with great teachers. His parents thought he was really odd but encouraged him all the same, loving him as their only son. As he grew older, he became popular for his political theories and in little time he worked his way up into becoming a top political voice. He became the Emperor of the Second French Empire and immediately set to work. He made policies that bettered the economy of his country, promoting business and sport. He made France a modern empire and saw to the innovation of infrastructure and technology. With time, France became a global authority again and everyone praised Louis Napoleon for his great service as emperor.

VOCABULARY

L'empereur - Emperor
Histoires - Stories
Contes - Tales
Bizarre - Odd
Travail - Work
Innovation - Innovation
Triste - Sad
Exploits - Exploits
Sport - Sports
Parié - Bettered
Promouvoir - Promote
Économie - Economy
Sociale - Social
Technologie - Technology
Encore - Again

COMPREHENSION QUESTIONS

Quelle était la motivation de Napoléon ? What was Napoleon's motivation?

Quelle a été l'attitude de ses parents face à son intérêt ? What was his parent's attitude towards his interest?

Comment Napoléon s'est-il comporté en tant qu'empereur ? How did Napoleon do as emperor?

HISTORICAL NOTE

The Second French Empire was a period of imperial rule by Napoleon III who had placed himself in power by force. This period is marked by significant economic and infrastructural growth and allowed France to reassert itself as a dominant power in Europe.

LES PRINCES INDIGNES

L'empereur Napoléon III entre en guerre avec la Confédération de l'Allemagne du Nord, mais ne parvient pas à gagner la guerre jusqu'à la fin de son règne. La France continue à se battre contre la guerre et à se disputer pour savoir qui va gouverner le pays. Le pays est devenu une république et ses dirigeants ont décidé de rétablir la monarchie. Trois personnes, Philippe, Charles et Louis, sont nommées au poste de roi de France. On leur fait passer un test pour déterminer qui est le meilleur, mais ils obtiennent tous les trois la même note. Incapables de se décider, on leur demande de combattre un guerrier pour mesurer leur force physique, mais ils tombent tous les trois à la renverse dès qu'ils voient le guerrier. On leur a demandé de gravir une montagne, mais aucun d'entre eux n'a réussi à en faire la moitié. Enfin, les juges frustrés leur ont donné la tâche la plus simple. On leur donna de minuscules lapins à allaiter pendant une semaine, mais les trois lapins moururent en un jour. Les juges ont vu qu'aucun d'entre eux n'en était digne et ont décidé qu'il valait mieux continuer à diriger la société en tant que république

THE UNWORTHY PRINCELINGS

Emperor Napoleon III got into a war with the North German Confederation but could not win the war until the end of his reign. France continued to fight with war as well as internal dispute on who would govern the country. The country became a republic and the leaders of the republic decided to set up the monarchy again. Three individuals, Philip, Charles and Louis were nominated for the position of King of France. They were each given a test to determine who was better but all three of them scored the same. Unable to decide, they were each asked to fight a warrior as a gauge of their physical strength but they all fell down on their faces the moment they saw the warrior. They were each asked to climb up a mountain but none of them could make it halfway up. Finally, the frustrated judges gave them each the simplest of tasks. They were given tiny rabbits to nurse for a week but all three rabbits died in a day. The judges saw that none of them were worthy and decided it would be better to keep ruling the company as a republic

VOCABULARY

Gagner - Win
Règner - Reign
Différend - Dispute
Interne - Internal
Nommé- Nominated
Position - Position
Guerrier - Warrior
Montagne - Mountain
Escalade - Climb
Juges - Judges
Tâches - Tasks
Lapin - Rabbit
Mieux - Better
Force - Strength
Jauge - Gauge

COMPREHENSION QUESTIONS

Selon vous, que signifie chaque tâche ? What do you think each task means?

Comment les candidats se sont-ils comportés ? How did the candidates perform?

Quels ont été les résultats de ces tests ? What were the results of these tests?

HISTORICAL NOTE

France adopted a republican system of government following the collapse of the Second French Empire as a result of the Franco-Prussian War. The Third Republic was made up of a Chamber of Deputies and a Senate to form the legislature and a resident to serve as head of state. The early governments of the republic considered re-establishing the monarchy but were unable to settle on fitting terms.

JOAN LA SÉRIE

Joan était un membre du corps législatif de la Troisième République française. C'était un homme discret qui aimait rester en retrait. Il ne parlait jamais à ses collègues en dehors du travail, ce qui lui donnait l'air d'être orgueilleux. Les autres s'allient et l'excluent. Ils élaborent des plans pour l'écarter de la législature. Un jour, Joan les informa qu'il y aurait bientôt une grande guerre dans le monde et qu'ils devaient faire des alliances s'ils voulaient survivre. Tous se moquent de lui et le traitent de colporteur de fausses nouvelles. Mais il ne se décourage pas. Il parle à ses collègues les uns après les autres, les exhortant à tenir compte de sa position et à signer des accords favorables qui renforceraient les alliances avec d'autres pays. Ils finissent par l'écouter et concluent des alliances commerciales et politiques avec la Russie et la Grande-Bretagne. Quelques jours plus tard, la Première Guerre mondiale commençait et tous s'émerveillaient de la chance qu'ils avaient eue.

JOAN THE SEER

Joan was a member of the legislature in the French Third Republic. He was a quiet man who liked to keep to himself. He never spoke outside of work to his colleagues and this gave him the appearance of being proud. The others formed alliances and excluded him. They made plans to remove him from the legislature. One day, Joan informed them that there would soon be a great war in the world and that they needed to make alliances if they planned to survive. They all laughed at him and called him a peddler of false stories. However, he was not discouraged. He spoke with his colleagues one after the other, urging them to consider his stance and sign favorable agreements that would solidify the alliances with other countries. Eventually, they listened to him and made trade and political alliances with Russia and Great Britain. Few days later, the First World War started and they all marveled at how lucky they were.

VOCABULARY

Retiré - Removed
Silence - Quiet
Législature - Legislature
Garder - Keep
Collègue - Colleague
Commerce - Trade
Décourager - Discourage
Survivre - Survive
Projets - Plans
Colporteur - Peddler
Chanceux - Lucky
Informé - Informed
A l'extérieur - Outside

COMPREHENSION QUESTIONS

Comment Joan a-t-il convaincu ses collègues ? How did Joan win his colleagues over?

Pourquoi n'ont-ils pas écouté Joan dans un premier temps ? Why did they initially not listen to Joan?

En quoi les alliances leur ont-elles été bénéfiques ? How did the alliances benefit them?

HISTORICAL NOTES

Triple Entente is a term used to describe the informal alliance between Russia, The United Kingdom of Great Britain and Ireland and The French Third Republic during World War I. It served as a powerful opposition to the Triple Alliance of the German Empire, the Austro-Hungarian Empire and the Kingdom of Italy.

LE CŒUR REBELLE D'ELOISE

La nouvelle en ville est que la France appartient désormais à l'Allemagne nazie. C'était pendant la Seconde Guerre mondiale et la France avait subi une grande défaite. Et bien qu'elle soit encore légalement considérée comme un État indépendant, plus de la moitié de son territoire est occupée par l'Allemagne nazie. Les Français ont peur et se demandent jour et nuit quel sera leur sort dans le cadre de cette nouvelle "politique de collaboration". Mais personne n'ose s'exprimer. Sauf Eloïse. Eloïse est propriétaire d'une librairie et le soir, sa librairie sert de lieu de rencontre aux citoyens qui s'opposent à l'occupation. Ils écrivaient des lettres pour dénoncer les nazis et les affichaient dans toute la ville. Malheureusement, la librairie d'Eloïse a fait l'objet d'une descente de police et elle a été emmenée en prison. Elle s'en est allée avec joie, sûre que d'autres personnes poursuivraient son travail et finiraient par déclencher une révolution.

ELOISE'S REBELLIOUS HEART

The news in town was that France now belonged to Nazi Germany. It was during the Second World War and France had suffered a great defeat. And although it was still legally considered an Independent State, more than half of its territory was occupied by Nazi Germany. The French people were afraid and wondered day and night what their fate would be under this new "collaboration policy". However, nobody dared to speak out. Except Eloise. Eloise was the owner of a bookstore and at nights, her bookstore served as a meeting place for citizens who were against the occupation. They wrote letters to denounce the Nazis and posted them all around the city. Sadly, Eloise's bookstore was raided and she was taken to prison. She went away gladly, sure that other people would continue her work and eventually trigger revolution.

VOCABULARY

Actualités - News
Appartenir - Belong
Souffrir - Suffer
Légalement - Legally
Moitié - Half
Destin - Fate
Nuit - Night
Librairie - Bookstore
Sous - Under
Dénoncer - Denounce
Lettres - Letters
Prison - Prison
Déclencheur - Trigger
Raflé - Raided

COMPREHENSION QUESTIONS

Comment Eloïse a-t-elle vécu son arrestation ? How did Eloise feel about her arrest?

Pourquoi les gens avaient-ils peur ? Why were the people afraid?

Que pensait Eloïse de la situation ? What was Eloise's belief about the situation?

HISTORICAL NOTE

Vichy France was the French state ruled by Marshal Philippe Petain after Nazi Germany had taken over half of French territories during the Second World War. It adopted a policy of collaboration under coercion and was governed from Vichy, an unoccupied free zone.

LA RÉSISTANCE VERS LA LIBERTÉ

De nombreux Français ont fui avant la défaite de la France face à l'Allemagne nazie. Hors de France, ils se sont organisés en une résistance politique et ont œuvré pour la liberté de leur pays. Ils ont collaboré avec les rébellions à l'intérieur de la France en leur envoyant une aide financière. L'un d'entre eux était Paul. Paul s'est rendu à Londres pour étudier avant le début de la Seconde Guerre mondiale. Lorsqu'il a appris la défaite de son pays, il a commencé à écrire des lettres, suppliant ses compatriotes de résister aux forces allemandes. Il écrit aux alliés de son pays, mais ceux-ci ne lui prêtent aucune attention et ne se soucient pas de la situation. Cependant, il a continué à diffuser ses messages et les alliés ont été contraints par la communauté internationale d'agir. Ils attaquent les forces nazies et reprennent la plupart des territoires français.

RESISTANCE UNTO FREEDOM

Many French citizens had fled before the defeat of France by Nazi Germany. Outside of France, they organized themselves into a political resistance and worked towards the freedom of their country. They worked with rebellions inside France by sending financial aid. One of them was Paul. Paul traveled to London to study before the start of the Second World War. When he learned of the defeat of his country he started to write letters, pleading with his countrymen to resist the German forces. He wrote to allies of his country but they paid him no heed and did not care for the situation. However, he continued to broadcast his messages and the allies were forced by the international community to act. They attacked the Nazi forces and took back most of France's territories.

VOCABULARY

Citoyens - Citizens
Résister - Resist
Forcé - Force
Alliés - Ally
Voyageurs - Traveled
Fui - Fled
Messages - Messages
Écriture - Wrote
Résistance - Resistance
Vers - Towards
Liberté - Freedom
Apprentissage - Learned
Communauté - Community
Étude - Study

COMPREHENSION QUESTIONS

Pourquoi les alliés ont-ils apporté leur aide ? Why did the allies help?

Comment Paul a-t-il pris la nouvelle de la défaite de son pays ? How did Paul take the news of the defeat of his country?

Qu'a-t-il fait pour redresser la situation ? What did Paul do to rectify the situation?

HISTORICAL NOTE

Free France was a French government established in exile in London in June 1940 after the defeat of France. It fought against the Axis (Nazi Germany and allies). It also encouraged and supported resistance in Nazi-occupied France.

D'ENNEMIS À AMIS

Sous la Quatrième République française, les choses ont commencé à changer pour le mieux. La France a commencé à se remettre de sa défaite lors de la Seconde Guerre mondiale et à reconstruire son économie. Un jour, un ambassadeur d'Allemagne rendit visite au gouvernement français et demanda une coopération entre les deux pays, mais les membres du corps législatif français rejetèrent instantanément cette offre. Madame Marie était une députée et une femme prévoyante. Elle a convaincu les autres parlementaires d'examiner les conditions de l'alliance allemande. Elle pensait qu'il valait mieux avoir un tel pays comme allié que comme ennemi. La proposition de coopération de l'Allemagne a été acceptée et la France en a tiré des avantages économiques.

ENEMIES TO FRIENDS

During the French Fourth Republic, things began to change for the better. France started to recover from its defeat in World War II and to build its economy back. One day, an ambassador from Germany visited the French Government and requested for cooperation between the two countries but members of the French legislature instantly rejected this offer. Madam Marie was a parliament member and a woman with foresight. She convinced the other parliamentarians to consider the terms of Germany's alliance. She believed it would be better to have such a country as an ally than as an enemy. Germany's proposal of cooperation was accepted and France enjoyed economic benefits from it.

VOCABULARY

Pendant - During
Tel que - Such
Construire - Build
Immédiatement - Instantly
Offre - Offer
Proposition - Proposal
Coopération - Cooperation
Avantage - Advantage
Ambassadeur - Ambassador
Ennemi - Enemy
Demandé - Requested
Changement - Change
Femme - Woman
Prévoyance - Foresight
Visité - Visited

COMPREHENSION QUESTION

Quel a été le résultat de la coopération entre la France et l'Allemagne ? What did cooperation between France and Germany result in?

Quelle a été la décision initiale du parlement ? What was the initial decision by the parliament?

Seriez-vous d'accord avec la coopération si vous étiez un parlementaire français ? Would you agree to cooperation if you were a French parliamentarian?

HISTORICAL NOTE

The French Fourth Republic was a time of tremendous economic growth in France. It focused mainly on the rebuilding of social institutions and industry after the Second World War and the fostering of international cooperation, even with former enemies. It was nonetheless a very unstable political era and it witnessed 21 administrations in a 12 year period.

GRANDE NATION, GRAND PEUPLE

Au cœur de l'Afrique, les populations commencent à réclamer leur indépendance. Ils en ont assez d'être exploités au profit de la France. Un leader se lève au Sénégal. Il s'appelait Dike et ses discours passionnés incitaient les gens à agir. Ils organisent des manifestations et écrivent des lettres aux communautés internationales pour demander la fin du colonialisme et des réparations. Ne pouvant ignorer la situation, la Cour internationale de justice convoque une audience au cours de laquelle les représentants de la France et du Sénégal défendront leurs positions. Dike est choisi comme représentant du Sénégal. Il s'exprime avec éloquence et passion, exposant les faits de l'affaire. À la fin de l'audience, qui a duré une semaine entière, l'indépendance a été accordée au Sénégal.

GREAT NATION, GREAT PEOPLE

In the heart of Africa, people began to clamor for independent rule. They were tired of being exploited for France's benefit. A leader rose up in Senegal. His name was Dike and his passionate speeches charged the people towards actions. They staged protests and wrote letters to the international communities, calling for the end of colonialism and reparations. Unable to ignore the situation, the International Court of Justice called for a hearing where representatives of France and Senegal would argue for their positions. Dike was chosen as the representative from Senegal. He spoke eloquently and with great passion, stating the facts of the case. At the end of the hearing that lasted a full week, Independence was awarded to Senegal.

VOCABULARY

Le cœur - Heart
Clameur - Clamor
Protestation - Protest
Fatigué - Tired
Représentants - Representatives
Passionnés - Passionate
Cas - Case
Situation - Situation
Leader - Leader
Éloquent - Eloquently
Exploité - Exploited
Discours - Speeches
Réparations - Reparations

COMPREHENSION QUESTIONS

Que voulaient les citoyens ? What did the people want?

De quelle manière les citoyens ont-ils fait entendre leur voix ? In what ways did the people make their voices heard?

Comment Dike a-t-il obtenu l'indépendance de son pays ? How did Dike gain independence for his country?

HISTORICAL NOTE

The decolonization movement of French colonies started in Algeria with demonstrations in May 1945, closely followed by Unrest in Haiphong and the Malagasy Uprising in Madagascar in 1947. Each of these movements saw the death of large numbers of native people but did not serve as enough of a deterrent.

COURTIER DE LA PAIX

Deux États membres des Nations unies sont engagés dans un conflit foncier. Le conflit a rapidement dégénéré en combats ouverts qui ont entraîné la perte de nombreuses vies humaines et la destruction de biens de part et d'autre. En tant que membre du Conseil de sécurité des Nations unies, la France a envoyé deux agents, Collins et Camille, pour enquêter sur la situation dans les pays en guerre. Les agents ont traversé d'innombrables épreuves et risqué leur vie pour entrer dans les pays. Ils ont découvert que ce sont d'autres grandes nations qui parrainent les guerres dans ces pays et ont fait part de leurs conclusions. La France a convoqué une réunion d'urgence du Conseil de sécurité et a présenté ses conclusions au Conseil. Le Conseil a sanctionné les pays membres qui parrainaient les guerres et celles-ci ont immédiatement pris fin.

PEACE BROKER

Two member states of the United Nations were locked in a land dispute. The dispute soon broke into open fighting that resulted in the loss of many lives and the destruction of property on both sides. As a member of the United Nations Security Council, France sent two agents, Collins and Camille to investigate the situation in the warring countries. The agents went through untold hardships and risked their lives to get into the countries. They found out that it was other bigger nations that were sponsoring the wars in these countries and reported their findings. France called an emergency Security Council meeting and tabled its findings before the council. The Council sanctioned the member countries sponsoring the wars and the wars came to an immediate end.

VOCABULARY

État - State
Bloqué - Locked
Litige - Dispute
Agent - Agent
Enquêter - Investigate
Inconnu - Untold
Propriété - Property
Conseil - Council
Nation - Nation
Sanction - Sanction
Parrainage - Sponsor
Perte - Loss
Destruction - Destruction

COMPREHENSION QUESTIONS

À quelle organisation la France appartenait-elle ? To what organization did France belong?

Comment la France a-t-elle enquêté sur le différend ? How did France investigate the dispute?

Quelles mesures ont été prises pour mettre fin à la guerre ? What steps were taken to end the war?

HISTORICAL NOTE

The United Nations and its Security Council were created after World War II to mitigate the failure of the League of Nations at fostering world peace. Since then France has been a permanent member in its Security Council.

Conclusion

Learning the basics of any language is difficult, and the French language can feel daunting for many newcomers. With that being said, if you were able to finish all of the lessons in this book, you have built a solid foundation in French.

However, learning a language is a long process that rewards consistency. Even just listening and watching French shows for 30 minutes a day can go a long way in improving your French skills. We sincerely hope that you continue your French language journey with the foundation you have built up and reach your goals, whether that be to understand the basics or speak like a native.

Thank you for choosing our book along your path to French mastery and we hope that you obtained a lot of useful information! If you have any questions, comments, or even suggestions we would love to hear from you by email at Contact@worldwidenomadbooks.com. We greatly appreciate the feedback and this allows us to improve our books and provide the best language learning experience we can.

Thank you,

Worldwide Nomad Team

Made in the USA
Coppell, TX
25 October 2024

39169616R00162